The Fascinating World of
Butterflies & Moths

The Fascinating World of
Butterflies & Moths

Bob Gibbons

NEW LINE BOOKS

'For Melissa –
the fairest butterfly of all'

This edition published by New Line Books.

Fax: (888) 719-7723 -- USA
e-mail: info@newlinebooks.com

Visit us on the web!
www.newlinebooks.com

ISBN: 1-59764-198-7

Printed and bound in China

**All photographs reproduced by kind permission of
Ardea London Limited.**

Page 2: **Comma butterfly** *Polygonia c-album*
Page 3: **Adonis Blue butterfly** *Lysandra bellargus*
Right: **Scarlet Tiger moth** *Callimorpha dominula*

Contents

Introduction

The vast group of butterflies and moths, collectively known as Lepidoptera (scaley wings), contain some of the most colourful creatures in the world, and they are undoubtedly among the most popular of insects. Altogether, there are over 165,000 known species of butterflies and moths in the world – and probably many more yet to be discovered or named – of which the great majority occur in the tropics. This book can, of course, do little more than provide an introduction to this vast group of species, but it does portray types from a wide range around the world, and attempts to show the great variety of forms that exist.

Butterflies and moths share many characteristics; so what is it that makes them different from each other? A common perception is that butterflies fly by day while moths fly at night and, while this is generally true, there are too many day-flying moths for this to be a very useful distinction. In fact, it is a difficult line to draw, as the relationship between the two groups is very close and rather arbitrary. Generally speaking, there are a range of characteristics which can provide more accurate categorization. For example, if the insect flies mainly by night and is attracted to bright lights, it is almost certainly a moth; if it flies by day it could be either. If the antennae are clubbed – that is, slender up as far as their extremities, where there is a sudden swelling – then it is

almost certainly a butterfly. A few moths have swollen tips to their antennae, such as the burnet moths (*see* p. 103), but they are less definitely clubbed. Most butterflies, when they roost, fold their wings vertically above their heads so that they resemble a flat leaf in shape. Moths have a variety of ways of holding their wings, but a few species do hold them in similar ways to butterflies. There are other technical differences, but these three distinctions will serve as a rough guide to distinguish one group from the other.

Butterflies and moths have the most fascinating life-cycles. We all have childhood memories of the magical transformation of a drab caterpillar, or even an inert chrysalis, into a beautiful, colourful butterfly. It is one of the most extraordinary metamorphisms in nature, designed to safeguard as many individuals as possible. Butterflies are delicate and vulnerable creatures, subject to predation by birds, other insects, spiders and so on, and susceptible to winter cold in less temperate parts of the world. Their complex life history exists to ensure that the species survive and the process of evolution continues.

The cycle could be said to begin with the egg. These are tiny tough-shelled structures containing the embryonic butterfly and are deposited by the adult female on or near a suitable foodplant. The eggs may be laid singly or in batches,

depending on the type of plant and the part of the plant the developing caterpillar is likely to consume. If, for example, it feeds on the fruits, and these are in shorter supply than usual, then only a few eggs will be laid. By contrast, a Large White butterfly (*see* p. 23), choosing her favourite foodplant, will lay a large batch on a nice fat cabbage with its abundance of leaves on which the caterpillars can feed.

The egg hatches into a larva or caterpillar which grows steadily, feeding on the foodplant, and regularly changing its skin. Each time it does so it enters into a new phase, or instar, and it may change colour as this occurs. Quite often the young larvae are very different from the older ones, perhaps for reasons of camouflage. Caterpillars may live for just a few weeks, or for many months, and in some species overwintering takes place in the caterpillar stage. The whole process depends on temperature, the type of foodplant, and the particular strategy of the species.

Eventually the caterpillar becomes fully grown, stops feeding, and finds somewhere to pupate – that is, to form a pupa or chrysalis. The pupal stage is the time when the internal parts of the insect are completely re-organized, changing it from a squat eating machine (the caterpillar) to an elegant, dispersing, mating machine – the adult butterfly. To achieve this incredible transformation the insect needs a great deal of protection because it will be totally immobile for a long period. Consequently, the pupal cases are often very solid, well-camouflaged, and frequently buried in the soil or in leaf litter where hungry predators are least likely to find them. Many species pass the winter as pupae because they are so well-protected from outside conditions, though this is by no means the only strategy: other species pass the winter as eggs, caterpillars, adults, or as a combination of these.

Eventually, the internal transformation is complete and the new butterfly emerges. In tropical areas the cycle of metamorphosis is rapid and depends solely on the amount of time it takes the caterpillar to eat enough, and how long it takes for the internal re-organization to take place. In temperate areas, though, the timing of the emergence is more critical and is linked to the onset of warmer weather, the growth of larval foodplants, and the availability of nectar flowers for the adults. The adult butterflies or moths will mate soon after emergence. The males, being usually more mobile, will seek out the females, though this is by no means always the case. In moths, this is particularly marked, and males often have very highly developed sense organs on their antennae to help them detect the presence of the more sedentary females which could be several miles away. In some instances, the females are completely flightless and simply wait for the males to find them.

Once mating has taken place the females will seek out foodplants, using all their senses to ensure that suitable ones are selected. This is crucial to the survival of most species; if the eggs are laid on the wrong foodplant, the young caterpillars will die: the females are rarely mistaken in their choice, and the whole cycle starts again. Most adult moths and butterflies feed, not to grow, but to maintain their energy levels for breeding, egg-laying and flight. It is in its adult phase that the insect colonizes new sites, and energy and mobility are critical to the accomplishment of this task. In fact, it is surprising how much variation there is between species in this respect. Many butterflies are quite sedentary and will only move a few hundred yards in the course of their adult life. Such insects tend to form discrete colonies which may evolve into slightly different races and which are very vulnerable to extinction if conditions were to suddenly change. In contrast, there are certain types of butterflies and moths which will migrate for hundreds, or even thousands of miles when conditions are right. Such species have less variation as they are constantly intermixing; they are also less likely to die out because they will always be able to find suitable new sites. They may, however, be vulnerable at their hibernation sites when thousands or millions may be gathered together in one place. An outbreak of fire at such a location would obviously be devastating.

All butterflies and moths have a very short life span, so they have to keep reproducing successfully. They have no means of surviving short periods of adverse conditions; for example, a butterfly which depends on flowers of open woodland will simply perish if the wood becomes overgrown and shaded, unless it is mobile enough to find another site. Similarly, the need for different conditions at each stage of its life-cycle means that it demands a more complex set of conditions than other organisms do.

In recent decades, butterflies have declined dramatically in many parts of the world. Only a few have adapted to new conditions created by man; the remainder need unspoilt bogs, marshes, heaths, ancient woods, and other habitats with stability and an abundance of flowers. Sadly, such places are disappearing as the human population increases and man's ability to dominate his environment grows apace. At least the needs of butterflies, moths and other creatures are now being better understood, and more nature reserves are being set aside for their protection. Unfortunately, however, the tide may be running in the other direction. These fascinating and complex creatures are worth protecting, not only for their own sake but for their ethereal beauty which we all enjoy.

Butterflies

PAPILIONIDAE

Common Swallowtail or Old World Swallowtail
Papilio machaon

Family: Papilionidae

Habitat: Lightly wooded areas, scrub, mountainsides and marshes, though it may be found almost anywhere, being highly mobile.

Distribution: Widely distributed through most of North America (south of the Hudson Bay), throughout Europe (though very rare in Britain), in northern Africa, and across temperate Asia as far as Japan.

Description: A large and colourful butterfly with a wingspan of 70–100mm ($2^{3}/_{4}$–4 inches). The ground colour is yellowish-cream, heavily marked with black on the forewings, while the hindwings have a band of shiny blue and a single large red spot. Each hindwing has a distinctive black 'tail'.

Life-cycle: The globular yellowish eggs are laid singly and soon turn brown before hatching into tiny black and white larvae, resembling bird droppings. As the larva grows it develops a beautiful striped coloration with black stripes, spotted with red, on a greenish background. Depending on the warmth of the climate, there may be one, two or three broods in a year, between April and September.

Larval Foodplants: In Europe, the foodplants belong exclusively to the umbellifers and include fennel, wild carrot and milk parsley; in North America, the foodplants include composites such as arctic sagebrush as well as members of the carrot family.

General Remarks: The only true swallowtail to have a circumpolar range, and the only one to occur in Britain at all, where it is confined to the fens of East Anglia. It has a powerful flight and alights frequently to feed at flowers.

Scarce Swallowtail *Iphiclides podalirius*

Family: Papilionidae

Habitat: Open countryside, especially where there is scrub or scattered light woodland.

Distribution: This species demands more warmth than the Common Swallowtail, occurring across Europe south of Britain and Scandinavia, and across temperate Asia as far as China. It does not extend into North America.

Description: A large butterfly, with a wingspan of 65–82mm ($2^{1}/_{2}$–$3^{1}/_{4}$ inches). Although broadly similar to the Common Swallowtail in size and colouring, it is distinguishable in that the forewings are strongly striped (rather than mottled) with black, the hindwings are striped (but less boldly), and it has a long yellow-tipped 'tail'.

Life-cycle: The eggs are laid singly on the stems of the foodplant, soon hatching and quickly developing into squat green caterpillars, lightly striped with yellow and dotted with red. In the northern part of its range, there are two generations per year, in April to June and August to September, but further south there are three broods, and it may be on the wing throughout the summer. The ground colour of the first brood of the year is a deeper yellow than subsequent ones.

Larval Foodplants: Blackthorn (*Prunus spinosa*) is the main foodplant, though other shrubs and small trees from the rose family, including cultivated fruit trees, may be used.

General Remarks: A strong and active flier, covering wide areas of countryside.

Southern Festoon *Zerynthia polyxena*

Family: Papilionidae

Habitat: Rough, stony, sunny locations where there are plenty of flowers, mainly in the lowlands, up to an altitude of about 1000m (3,300ft).

Distribution: Its stronghold is in south-eastern Europe, from the extreme south-east of France eastwards and extending into western Asia. It is particularly common in Greece, Turkey and adjacent areas.

Description: A medium-sized butterfly with a wingspan of 45–55mm (1³⁄₄–2 inches), boldly marked with black on yellow, and with a series of red spots, especially on the hindwings. Close to the margin of each wing is a conspicuous black zig-zag line, giving the appearance of a fringed border.

Life-cycle: The eggs are laid, often in large numbers, on the low-growing foodplants. The caterpillars are pale brown to grey, covered in short, thick, reddish spikes, while the pupae are slender, brownish and supported in an erect position on the stems. There is only one generation per year, in April or May.

Larval Foodplants: The only known foodplants are the birthworts, or Dutchman's pipes (*Aristolochia* spp.), and these may be seen in favoured localities in May and June, covered with caterpillars.

General Remarks: A rather sedentary butterfly, tending to occur in loose colonies rather than spreading widely. It has declined in recent years due to changes in agricultural practices.

11

Apollo *Parnassius apollo*

Family: Papilionidae

Habitat: Almost invariably found in mountain areas (although it occurs in equivalent habitats closer to sea level in arctic areas), where it favours grassy locations with an abundance of flowers, often on limestone up to 2000m (6600ft) or so.

Distribution: The Apollo occurs throughout Europe, wherever there are sizeable mountains (though it is absent from Britain), and across Asia as far east as Mongolia. There are closely related species in the Himalayas and the mountains of China.

Description: A large and distinctive butterfly, with a wingspan of 70–80mm ($2^3/_4$–$3^1/_4$ inches). The ground colour is creamy-white (often more greyish in the female), boldly marked with a few large black spots on the forewings, and red spots edged with black on the hindwings (though there are many slightly different races throughout the range).

Life-cycle: The eggs are laid in summer on the foodplants and may either remain as eggs over winter, or hatch into caterpillars in autumn but remain small until spring. The caterpillars are deep brown marked with red, and they feed almost exclusively in sunny weather. There is only one generation per year, flying from June to September depending on altitude and locality.

Larval Foodplants: The caterpillars feed on related species of succulents in the stonecrop (*Sedum*) and houseleek family.

General Remarks: A very beautiful butterfly which has suffered badly at the hands of collectors and from agricultural changes to its habitats. Protected by law in many countries.

Blue Triangle or Common Bluebottle Butterfly
Graphium sarpedon

Family: Papilionidae

Habitat: Open sunny locations with abundant flowers such as parks, gardens, and forest margins and clearings.

Distribution: This beautiful butterfly can be seen in much of southern Asia, including India, Malaysia, China, Japan and Sri Lanka. It also occurs southwards through Papua New Guinea and the Solomons into Australia.

Description: A large butterfly, with a wingspan of 80–90mm (3$^1/_4$–3$^1/_2$ inches). The wings are a dark velvety-black, characterized by a bold, interrupted blue or greenish band running across the forewings on both upper and lower surfaces, forming a triangle at the point closest to the body. The colour fades almost to white in older specimens. The hindwings have several greenish or blue crescents close to the margins.

Life-cycle: The caterpillars have three pairs of spines on the body just behind the head, and they feed solitarily on the foodplant. In warmer tropical and subtropical areas, the butterfly is on the wing for most of the year, flying swiftly between flowers or patches of mud.

Larval Foodplants: A variety of foodplants from several different families are used, including myrtles, laurels and others.

General Remarks: In some areas of Australia, the caterpillars can be a small-scale pest of the camphor laurel (*Cinnamomum* spp.).

Orchard Swallowtail *Papilio aegeus*

Family: Papilionidae

Habitat: Most frequent in and around parks and gardens, though sometimes occurs in lightly wooded areas.

Distribution: Common in populated areas of Australia, and northwards into Papua New Guinea and nearby tropical islands.

Description: A large butterfly, with a wingspan of 75–90mm (3–3½ inches). The forewings are velvety-black with a few white spots close to the front margins; the hindwings have a large central patch of yellowish-white broadly edged with black. There are no 'tails' on the hindwings, unlike most swallowtails.

Life-cycle: The caterpillars feed singly on the leaves of the foodplant and resemble bird-droppings when young, which probably allows them to escape predation. As they grow, they develop either dark brown stripes or dull white stripes. The number of broods vary according to temperature, and in the more northern parts of its range it is on the wing all year round.

Larval Foodplants: Species of *Citrus* such as oranges and lemons. They occur in areas of cultivated fruits, but rarely in large enough numbers to be considered pests.

General Remarks: Frequently seen in areas where there are abundant flowers.

Common Rose Swallowtail
Pachliopta aristolochiae

Family: Papilionidae

Habitat: Occurs in a wide range of habitats including flowery grasslands, open forests, parks and gardens. It is a very mobile species and can occur almost anywhere within its range, up to an altitude of about 1200m (3960ft).

Distribution: Confined to Asia, in a broad band from India eastwards through the lower Himalayas, Burma, South China and southwards into Malaysia.

Description: A large butterfly with a wingspan of 80–110mm ($3\frac{1}{4}$–$4\frac{1}{3}$ inches), it has a fat, red furry body; the forewings are creamy-white, veined with black, with black at the bases and margins. The hindwings are a more complex pattern of black with white patches and red dots, with distinct black 'tails', though there are many different races in which the red or white may be either more marked or absent altogether.

Life-cycle: This species can occur at virtually any time of year through most parts of its range. The caterpillars feed on poisonous plants, absorbing the toxin which is transferred to the adult butterflies. Their bright colours serve as a warning to predators, and they are generally avoided.

Larval Foodplants: Members of the genus *Aristolochia*, including wild species such as *A. indica*; but it also breeds on cultivated species in parks and gardens.

General Remarks: May migrate in some parts of the range, and pass the winter in large communal roosts, often accompanied by the closely-related Crimson Rose.

Common Mormon *Papilio polytes*

Family: Papilionidae

Habitat: Most frequent in and around parks and gardens, though it may also occur on agricultural land and along forest margins.

Distribution: From India, eastwards across south-east Asia into China and Japan, and southwards as far as the Philippines.

Description: A large butterfly with a wingspan of 90–100mm (3$\frac{1}{2}$–4 inches), it is a complicated butterfly to describe because, not only do males and females differ markedly, but there are also three different forms of the female, mimicking other species. Males are largely black, with rows of creamy spots on the hindwings, and black 'tails'. Females normally have much more red and white in their make-up, resembling either the Common Rose or Crimson Rose Swallowtail, though one form is very similar to the male of this species.

Life-cycle: The caterpillars initially resemble bird-droppings, but gradually become greener through their later instars. Adults are on the wing for most of the year.

Larval Foodplants: Particularly fond of cultivated *Citrus* plants, especially orange (*C. sinensis*), and lime (*C. aurantifolia*), although they also feed on the curry-leaf plant and some wild species of *Rutacea*.

General Remarks: This attractive butterfly has adapted strongly to urban life and is now much more common around habitations than it is in more natural settings.

Great Mormon *Papilio memnon*

Family: Papilionidae

Habitat: Based mainly around wooded areas, the females tend to stay close to trees while males wander further abroad and can be frequently seen in parks and gardens, visiting flowers.

Distribution: Southern Asia, from India and Sri Lanka eastwards to China and Japan, and southwards into the Philippines.

Description: A very large butterfly, with a wingspan of 120–150mm (4¾–6 inches). The males are reasonably consistent in colour, being almost entirely blue-black, with indistinct greyish stripes; the hindwings are scalloped on the margins, but there are no 'tails'. The females, however, vary considerably and mimic a range of other species, including the Common Rose and one of the birdwing butterflies; essentially, they have dark forewings marked with broad creamy-yellow stripes, while the hindwings are heavily marked with white and red and there are distinct black 'tails' in some forms.

Life-cycle: As with many swallowtails, the caterpillars resemble bird-droppings when young, becoming green later. The adults are on the wing for most of the year, except winter, in the more northern parts of its range.

Larval Foodplants: A wide variety of forest shrubs, such as species of *Glycosmis*.

General Remarks: A common and attractive species and a familiar visitor to gardens over most of its range. In temperate areas it is frequently kept in butterfly houses.

Citrus Swallowtail *Papilio demodocus*

Family: Papilionidae

Habitat: A common visitor to a wide range of sunny, open habitats with abundant flowers, it is a very mobile species that can occur almost anywhere within its range.

Distribution: Widespread through southern Africa, with the exception of desert areas.

Description: A large butterfly, with a wingspan of 90–120mm ($3\frac{1}{2}$–$4\frac{1}{4}$ inches). Males and females are similar in pattern, though the females are larger; the forewings are blackish, dotted and speckled with white, while the underwings are similar with the addition of two eye-spots on each wing. Unlike many swallowtails, there are no tails to the wings of either sex. The undersides of the wings are similar, though slightly paler.

Life-cycle: The eggs are singly laid and hatch into caterpillars that resemble bird-droppings for their first few instars. Later they become greener, and (like other swallowtail caterpillars) have an organ that can be protruded when they are threatened which emits a powerful citrus-like odour. In most parts of its range, and during summer only, there are one or two broods, though in the warmest parts, such as the eastern coast, they may be on the wing all year.

Larval Foodplants: The larvae feed on a wide range of plants, particularly the various species *Citrus* (as the common name suggests), and members of the species *Rutacea*, in addition to other herbs and shrubs.

General Remarks: An active and attractive species, of which the males are territorial and fond of visiting flowers and mud puddles.

Pale Swallowtail *Papilio eurymedon*

Family: Papilionidae

Habitat: Occurs in a wide range of open habitats, including open woodland, chaparral, hilltops and river valleys.

Distribution: A species of western North America, extending from British Columbia southwards to Baja California, and eastwards as far as Montana and western Texas.

Description: A largish butterfly, with a wingspan of 70–88mm ($2^3/_4$–$3^1/_2$ inches), it is typical of most swallowtails in general shape and colouring; the upper sides of the wings are black with white markings, roughly in the form of a broad 'V', spreading out into further stripes on the forewings. There is a single long slender tail on each hindwing. The undersides are similar, though paler.

Life-cycle: Initially, the larvae are black-and-white, but soon turn green as they mature. Depending on the climate there may be one or two generations per year, from April to July. They overwinter as dark brown pupae.

Larval Foodplants: The larvae feed on a variety of shrubby plants, including coffee-berry and other plants of the species buckthorn (*Rhamnus*), various species of *Ceanothus*, and some species of cherry and plum.

General Remarks: Darker, high-altitude forms occur in some mountain ranges which are considered by some to be a subspecies.

Zelicaon or Anise Swallowtail *Papilio zelicaon*

Family: Papilionidae

Habitat: Mobile and wide-ranging through a variety of more open habitats, such as fields, waste ground, roadsides, open hillsides, gardens and open woodlands.

Distribution: Primarily a species of the western United States, from British Columbia southwards to the Mexican border, and in a narrow band eastwards to the Great Lakes. Occurs locally in Mexico.

Description: A large butterfly, with a wingspan of 70–85mm ($2^3/_4$–$3^1/_3$ inches). The upper surfaces are blackish, with a single very broad yellow stripe across both wings which expands downwards so that the hindwings are half yellow. There is a red and blue eye-spot on each hindwing, and a single tail. The undersides are very similar, though rather paler.

Life-cycle: In its early stages the caterpillars resemble black-and-white bird droppings, like many other swallowtail larvae; they become progressively greener with dark bands and yellow spots. In northern areas there is one brood per year, on the wing from April to July. Further south, there are several generations throughout the warmer months.

Larval Foodplants: Feeds on a variety of different members of the family *Umbellifera*, such as fennel and mountain parsley, and may feed on cultivated plants from this family if they occur in the right conditions.

General Remarks: There are other variants of these butterflies, grading into the much darker Nitra Swallowtail and the Gothic Swallowtail, which are sometimes treated as separate species, though genetically very similar.

Tiger Swallowtail or Eastern Tiger Swallowtail *Papilio glaucus* (pictured right)

Family: Papilionidae

Habitat: Broad-leaved woodlands, especially around their margins, and in parks and gardens.

Distribution: Most frequent in eastern North America, from the Canadian border southwards, and including Mexico. Absent from parts of the western United States.

Description: A large butterfly, though variable in size according to location, the females are larger than the males and wingspan is between 70 and 130mm ($2^3/_4$–$5^1/_8$ inches). The upper surfaces of the wings are mostly yellow, with black margins and black streaks towards the inner margins, ill-defined red and blue eye-spots on the hindwings, and single slender tails. Some forms are much darker and smaller than the typical specimens.

Life-cycle: The caterpillars are green and gradually develop pairs of large black-centred orange eye-spots in front of orange-and-black bars. The adults are on the wing between May and July in one generation towards the north of the range, but there may be up to three broods further south, on the wing between February and November.

Larval Foodplants: The larvae feed on a wide range of deciduous trees and shrubs from several different families among them willows, (*Salix* spp.), birches (*Betula* spp.), ashes (*Fraxinus* spp.), and cottonwoods (*Populus* spp.).

General Remarks: A widely-distributed and very variable species, grading into other species in the north of its range; there is some conjecture as to whether the Canadian Tiger Swallowtail and Arctic Tiger Swallowtail should be considered subspecies or separate species.

Butterflies

PIERIDAE

Black-Veined White *Aporia crataegi*

Family: Pieridae

Habitat: Occurs in open or semi-shaded hilly areas where there are abundant flowers, though it is very mobile and can turn up almost anywhere.

Distribution: A widely distributed butterfly, occurring throughout Europe (though only an occasional visitor to Britain and northern Scandinavia), and across most of temperate Asia.

Description: A medium-sized butterfly with a wingspan of 50–65mm (2–2$\frac{1}{2}$ inches). Although not particularly striking in appearance, the Black-Veined White can be readily identified by its combination of plain creamy-white ground colour and pattern of fine black lines on all wing surfaces.

Life-cycle: The caterpillars live gregariously in silken nests until after their winter hibernation when they separate out before pupating in spring. Adults emerge in May or June and are on the wing until July or August; there is only one generation per year.

Larval Foodplants: The main foodplants are shrubs and small trees of the family *Rosa*, such as hawthorn and blackthorn, though in southern areas it may become a pest, decimating apple and other fruit orchards.

General Remarks: This butterfly has declined markedly in the north of its range, though it is still abundant further south. In warm weather it often clusters in large numbers to drink in mineral salts on patches of wet ground.

Large White *Pieris brassicae*

Family: Pieridae

Habitat: Occurs in open, sunny and flowery habitats and is particularly common around gardens and cultivated areas.

Distribution: Common just about everywhere in Europe, including the far north, as well as in north Africa and across Asia as far as western China.

Description: Very similar in size to the Black-Veined White. The ground colour is off-white and the forewings have a boldly-marked black tip on the upper surfaces. Females have two large black spots and a stripe on their forewings. The undersides of the hindwings are plain, yellowish in the first brood, paler in later generations.

Life-cycle: The yellow bottle-shaped eggs are laid in batches of up to 100 on the undersides of leaves. The caterpillars become conspicuous, mottled grey-green with black blotches, feeding in large groups and often stripping their foodplants to skeletons. In northern parts of its range there are two broods per year, between April and October, though further south there may be several overlapping generations.

Larval Foodplants: Feeds on a range of species of the cabbage family, such as watercress (*Nasturtium officionale*), but is always most abundant on cultivated cabbages and their relatives, and also on garden nasturtiums (*Tropaeolum majus*).

General Remarks: An abundant species throughout its range, though often a pest of crops and in gardens. Migration northwards takes place each year, with a partial southwards migration in autumn.

Small White *Pieris rapae*

Family: Pieridae

Habitat: In flowery sunny places, especially near gardens and cultivated crops of the *Brassica* family. Abundant almost everywhere.

Distribution: Originally native primarily to Europe, north Africa and temperate Asia, this butterfly now occurs in many parts of the world through accidental introduction, including North America and Australia.

Description: A small to medium butterfly with a wingspan of 40–50mm (1½–2 inches). The colour and markings are very similar to those of the Large White, though less bold; the first generation each year is paler than the second.

Life-cycle: The yellowish conical eggs are laid singly (unlike the clusters of the Large White) on the undersides of leaves. The caterpillars are green, with yellow stripes along their sides, and they feed singly. Adults can be on the wing throughout the summer from April to October, with two broods in cooler areas, or three to four in warmer parts.

Larval Foodplants: Various members of the cabbage (*Brassica*) family, such as cress and particularly the cultivated varieties and their relatives. It can become a major pest of cabbages and similar crops.

General Remarks: One of the commonest butterflies in the world, and a widespread pest. Some migration northwards takes place, especially in years of high population growth.

Green-Veined White (U.K.) or Sharp-Veined or Mustard White (U.S.A.) *Pieris napi*

Family: Pieridae

Habitat: The Green-Veined White occurs in a wide variety of natural habitats, including open woodland, woodland rides, riversides, damp meadows, and occasionally gardens.

Distribution: Throughout Europe and across temperate Asia as far as Japan; widespread in temperate North America.

Description: A medium to small butterfly with a wingspan of 35–45mm ($1^{1}/_{3}$–$1^{3}/_{4}$ inches). The upper surfaces of the wings are rather similar to those of the Small White but with the veins more clearly defined; the undersides, however, are distinctive with broad greyish to greenish veins on a yellow background. Mountain races may be more darkly marked, appearing almost grey overall.

Life-cycle: The yellowish conical eggs are laid on the leaves of the foodplant, hatching into solitary green caterpillars. Overwintering always takes place in pupal form. The number of generations per year varies from one in cold areas to three in warmer conditions, though there are two generations in most places. The butterfly is on the wing between April and October.

Larval Foodplants: The caterpillars feed on cuckooflowers (*Cardamine pratensis*), watercress (*Nasturtium officionale*), and hedge mustard (*Sysimbrium officionale*); unlike the 'cabbage whites' (the Large and Small Whites), it does not feed on crops and is not a pest.

General Remarks: An attractive little butterfly, unfortunately often confused with its close relatives, the cabbage whites.

25

Bath White *Pontia daplidice* (pictured right)

Family: Pieridae

Habitat: Occurs in a wide variety of rough flowery habitats, from sea level up to 2000m (6600ft).

Distribution: Ranges across the whole of Europe and Asia as far as Japan, and also extends southwards into north Africa. Despite being named after the city of Bath, in England, it is only a very rare visitor to Britain. It is also one of the few butterflies to reach Iceland.

Description: A medium to small butterfly with a wingspan of 35–45mm ($1\frac{1}{3}$–$1\frac{3}{4}$ inches), it is similar in size to the Green-Veined White. Although the ground colour is white, it is heavily chequered with black and grey on the upper surfaces or suffused with green on the undersides. Females are normally more heavily marked than males.

Life-cycle: The eggs are laid singly on the leaves and stems of the foodplant, soon hatching into dark green caterpillars, striped longitudinally with orange-red. They may overwinter as caterpillars or pupae. In most parts of its range there are two generations per year, in spring and late summer, though in the warmest areas it breeds almost continuously from February until October.

Larval Foodplants: The main foodplants are various members of the cabbage family such as cress, though it also feeds on wild mignonette (*Reseda lutea*).

General Remarks: Bath Whites regularly migrate northwards each year, though they are not resident in more northerly regions.

Peak, Chequered or Common White *Pontia callidice* (pictured right)

Family: Pieridae

Habitat: Almost exclusively to be found in flowery alpine meadows, from 1500m (5000ft) up to about 2800m (9300ft).

Distribution: A widespread species occurring in mountain ranges of southern Europe (especially the French Alps and Pyrenees), across the temperate parts of Asia, and in North America, where it extends to mountain areas in different colour forms.

Description: Similar in size (35–45mm) and general appearance to the Bath White (left), it differs in quite small details such as the more pointed forewings and the line of 'arrow-head' marks on the undersides of the hindwings. It also lacks the roughly circular black spot on the forewing of the Bath White.

Life-cycle: The eggs are laid singly on the foodplants and the caterpillars are greenish-grey with paler lines and rows of warts. It overwinters in pupal form, hatching into the adult in midsummer. There is normally only one generation per year, thanks to the cold conditions prevalent in its habitat.

Larval Foodplants: The main larval food plants are types of treacle mustard (*Erysimum cheiranthoides*) and mignonettes (*Reseda lutea*).

General Remarks: A high mountain specialist, confined to relatively few locations scattered over a wide area.

Life-cycle: The eggs are laid singly among the flowers of the foodplant and eventually develop into slender green caterpillars with white stripes along their sides. The adults emerge in spring, usually April, flying until June, with only one generation a year.

Larval Foodplants: The foodplants are restricted to members of the cabbage family, especially the cuckooflower or lady's smock (*Cardamine pratensis*), garlic mustard (*Alliaria petiolata*), and rockets (*Sysimbrium* spp.), the caterpillars feeding on the flowers and buds rather than the leaves.

General Remarks: Specimens are occasionally found where the wings of one individual are differently marked, one with male colours, the other with female.

Orange Tip
Anthocharis cardamines

Family: Pieridae

Habitat: In damp meadows, open woods and woodland rides, or along hedgerows.

Distribution: Widespread throughout most of Europe, apart from the extreme north and far south-west; it also occurs across temperate Asia as far as Japan, where it is a slightly different sub-species.

Description: A medium to small butterfly with a wingspan of 35–45mm ($1\frac{1}{3}$–$1\frac{3}{4}$ inches). The females are rather similar to Bath Whites, though with less black on the forewings; the males; however, are very distinctive, the outer half of each forewing being strongly marked with orange – it is even visible through the wings when the butterfly has its wings closed.

Clouded Yellow *Colias croceus*

Family: Pieridae

Habitat: A mobile butterfly which can occur almost anywhere, it favours sunny locations of all kinds where there are abundant flowers.

Distribution: Throughout most of Europe, with the exception of the far north, and eastwards across Asia as far as Afghanistan. In the northern part of its range it occurs as a migrant only, failing to survive the winters.

Description: A medium to large butterfly with a wingspan of 40–50mm (1½–2 inches). The basic ground colour of the wings is yellow, ranging in tone from pale orange to lemon, each wing being broadly edged with black. There is usually an oval black spot in the centre of each forewing, and a white spot edged with pink on the underside of the hindwings.

Life-cycle: The bottle-shaped pinkish eggs are laid singly and hatch into greenish caterpillars with white stripes along their sides. They overwinter as caterpillars, rather than pupae, which may explain why they cannot survive winters further north. The number of generations per year varies, with two in the north of the range but three or more further south so that it is on the wing virtually all year round.

Larval Foodplants: Various members of the pea family such as clovers (*Trifolium* spp.) and vetches (*Vicia* spp.), though it does particularly well on lucerne (*Medicago sativa*), where it is planted as a fodder crop.

General Remarks: A strong migrant, travelling northwards in huge numbers in some years (such as 1996), it reaches areas where it has little hope of surviving the winter.

Brimstone *Gonepteryx rhamni*

Family: Pieridae

Habitat: Open woods, scrub, downland, fens and other rough floriferous locations.

Distribution: Widespread throughout virtually the whole of Europe, except the far north, and across the temperate parts of Asia as far as Japan, where a different race occurs.

Description: A medium to large butterfly, with a wingspan of 50–60mm (2–2$\frac{1}{3}$ inches). Male Brimstones are very distinctive being a beautiful deep, even, yellow, with no markings apart from a single orange spot on each wing; the tips of the forewings have distinctive triangular 'hooks', quite unlike the Whites and Clouded Yellows. Females are much paler and could be mistaken for Large Whites, though lacking in black markings.

Life-cycle: The yellowish eggs are laid singly in early summer on the leaves of the foodplant. The caterpillars are green with a single pale stripe, and by July they have pupated. The adults that emerge in late summer then hibernate, re-emerging to fly on warm winter days and becoming fully active in spring to mate and lay eggs for a new generation.

Larval Foodplants: Most frequently purging buckthorn (*Rhamnus catharticus*) or alder buckthorn (*Frangula alnus*), though privet (*Ligustrum vulgare*) and spindle (*Euonymus europaeus*) may be used.

General Remarks: The best contender for the name 'butterfly', with its striking appearance and butter-coloured wings.

African Migrant *Catopsilia florella*

Family: Pieridae

Habitat: This wide-ranging butterfly may occur in almost any flowery habitat, such as savannah, mountainside and unimproved grasslands.

Distribution: Occurs throughout Africa, south of the Sahara desert, and eastwards across the warmer parts of Asia as far as China. It has recently been recorded in the Canary Isles, where it appears to be spreading.

Description: A medium-sized butterfly, with a wingspan of 50–70mm (2–2$\frac{3}{4}$ inches), it bears some resemblance to the Clouded Yellows, but lacks the black tips to the wings. The males are a pale greenish-yellow with black spots on the forewings, while the females are an overall deeper yellow.

Life-cycle: In most parts of its range it flies for much of the year, producing continuous broods, and can be seen in flight in virtually any month of the year. It migrates strongly throughout Africa, according to weather conditions.

Larval Foodplants: Various species of cassia, such as *C. didymobotrya*.

General remarks: A fast-flying and conspicuous butterfly that is gradually extending its range. This is due to the fact that cassias are now being widely used as ornamental plants in gardens.

Australian Wood White *Delias aganippe*

Family: Pieridae

Habitat: Open woodland, scrub and areas of abundant flowering plants.

Distribution: Centred around South Australia, it extends northwards in favourable locations, according to conditions.

Description: A medium-sized butterfly, with a wingspan of 60–65mm ($2^{1}/_{3}$–$2^{1}/_{2}$ inches). The upper surfaces of the wings are yellowish-white, tipped with black and edged with black and white, and there is a black-and-white spot on the front edge of each forewing. The under surfaces have red spots around the margins of the hindwings and towards the base of the wings. Females are similar to males, but have more black on the wing margins.

Life-cycle: The eggs are laid in batches on the foodplant, and the caterpillars feed communally in silken webs suspended among the leaves. There is normally one generation per year, in summer.

Larval Foodplants: Various parasites of *Loranthaceae*, particularly *Amyema cambegei*.

General remarks: A common species throughout most of southern Australia.

Common Grass Yellow *Eurema hecabe*

Family: Pieridae

Habitat: In various open flowery locations, such as woodland clearings, meadows, gardens and parks.

Distribution: Common in the warmer parts of Asia, especially in the Indian sub-continent, where it is abundant and widespread. It also occurs in Australia.

Description: A small to medium-sized butterfly, with a wingspan of 40–50mm ($1\frac{1}{2}$–2 inches). The upper surfaces of the wings are bright yellow, with boldly-marked black tips to the forewings. The under surfaces are yellow, dotted and mottled with white and brown; males and females are similar but there are a number of closely-related species differing in small details of colour and pattern.

Life-cycle: In most parts of its range the butterfly is on the wing all year, continuously producing broods, though towards the edges of the range, such as in north India, it ceases to breed during the coolest periods of winter.

Larval Foodplants: The main foodplants are species of cassia, though English tamarind (*Pithecellobium dulce*), and various leguminous shrubs, such as albizzia, may also be used.

General remarks: A weak and erratic flyer, the butterfly can often be seen to drop suddenly down into the grass. It frequently visits flowers and drinks at the muddy edges of puddles during hot periods.

Butterflies

LYCAENIDAE

Purple Hairstreak *Quercusia quercus*

Family: Lycaenidae

Habitat: Mostly confined to mature woodland with oaks, or areas where large numbers of old oaks occur.

Distribution: Throughout most of Europe except for the northern parts of Scandinavia, and eastwards into Asia as far as Armenia.

Description: A small butterfly, with a wingspan of 30–35mm ($1\frac{1}{4}$–$1\frac{1}{3}$ inches). The upper surfaces of the wings, particularly in the males, are a lovely deep purple, iridescent according to the angle of view. The under wings are silvery-grey with a rambling white streak and an orange spot. The hindwings have short triangular tails.

Life-cycle: The eggs resemble flat greyish discs, laid singly near the flower buds, and it is in this form that overwintering takes place. The caterpillars are brown, rather like woodlice in shape, and feed mainly at night. The single generation of adults emerge in June or July and fly until August or September.

Larval Foodplants: The commonest foodplant is the oak, though ash may occasionally be used.

General Remarks: An unusual butterfly in that it spends most of its time among tree-tops, rarely venturing to ground level, and is often overlooked as a result.

White-Letter Hairstreak *Strymonidia w-album*

Family: Lycaenidae

Habitat: Open woodland or forest clearings; also in hedges and other places where elms occur.

Distribution: Occurs throughout central Europe but is largely absent from the Iberian peninsula and from much of Scandinavia. It occurs right across the temperate zone of Asia as far as Japan.

Description: Similar in size and general shape to the Purple Hairstreak, its general ground colour is a dark, greyish-brown, the upper surfaces of the wings being unremarkable; however, on the undersides there is a white zig-zag line which usually forms a clear 'W' on the hindwings – hence its name. The hindwings also have strong bands of orange a little way in from the margin and long white-tipped black 'tails'.

Life-cycle: The greyish disc-shaped eggs are singly laid in summer, hatching in the following spring to produce green woodlice-shaped caterpillars. The adults emerge in June, and the single generation flies for a brief time until early August.

Larval Foodplants: Mainly elm (*Ulmus* spp.), though other deciduous trees may be used. The adult butterflies are particularly fond of feeding at bramble flowers (*Rubus fructosus*), and other nectar-rich plants such as hemp-agrimony (*Eupatorium cannabinum*) are visited.

General Remarks: This species has suffered a serious decline in many areas due to the wholesale destruction of elms by Dutch Elm disease. There are now signs of a modest recovery.

Green Hairstreak *Callophrys rubi*

Family: Lycaenidae

Habitat: Occurs in a wider variety of habitats than any other butterfly, thanks to its wide choice of foodplants. It is seen most frequent in bogs, moorlands, mountains, coastal grasslands and scrub, though it may also occur in open woodland, meadows or on chalk downland.

Distribution: Widespread throughout Europe, it occurs in north Africa and across temperate Asia to the Pacific.

Description: One of the smallest hairstreaks, with a wingspan of little more than 24–28mm (1–1$\frac{1}{8}$ inches). Its distinctive feature, unlike any other European butterfly, is the almost uniform metallic green of the undersides of both wings which occurs in both sexes. The upper surfaces of the wings are a dull brown, the butterfly appearing totally brown in flight and showing its brighter colours only when settling.

Life-cycle: The greenish glassy eggs are laid singly and soon hatch into green woodlice-shaped caterpillars. These pupate in late summer and pass the winter in this form. There may be one or two generations, depending on climate, and adults are on the wing between March and August.

Larval Foodplants: The range of foodplants is remarkably wide and includes species from many different families. Among the most common are: bilberry (*Vaccinium myrtillus*), gorse (*Ulex europaeus*), broom (*Cytisus scoparius*), dyer's greenweed (*Genista tinctoria*), rock-rose (*Helianthemum* spp.), bird's foot trefoil (*Lotus corniculatus*), dogwood (*Cornus sanguinea*), heathers (*Erica* spp.) and various others.

General Remarks: The males are territorial and will defend a favoured sunny perch against other males.

Large Copper *Lycaena dispar*

Family: Lycaenidae

Habitat: Fens, marshes and damp grassland.

Distribution: Patchily distributed in Europe from France eastwards, and also occurring sporadically across Asia to the Pacific. It became extinct in England in about 1847, though it has been reintroduced (as a different race, from Holland) since, and just manages to survive in small numbers.

Description: A beautiful intense orange predominates the upper surfaces of the wings, which have a span of 30–40mm (1$\frac{1}{4}$–1$\frac{1}{2}$ inches), each being finely edged in black; however, the females are rather more strongly marked with brownish-black, especially on the hindwings. The undersides of the hindwings, visible when the insect is at rest, are a light grey, dotted with black with an orange stripe.

Life-cycle: The eggs are singly laid in late summer and soon hatch into caterpillars. They overwinter as partially-grown larvae which can survive flooding of their wetland habitat. They pupate in early summer and the adults emerge in June or July. Occasionally, if conditions are favourable, there may be more than one generation.

Larval Foodplants: Various docks, especially the great water dock (*Rumex hydrolapathum*).

General Remarks: A number of different races of this species occur, though all are declining through drainage of their wetland habitat.

37

Long-Tailed Blue (or Pea, Bean and Lucerne Blue) *Lampides boeticus*

Family: Lycaenidae

Habitat: Most frequently found in rough flowery conditions, though also occurring in areas of agriculture, open woodland, and on mountainsides.

Distribution: A widely-distributed butterfly, it is unusual in that it occurs both in tropical and temperate areas. Its range includes much of Europe apart from the north, most of Africa and Asia, many Pacific islands including Hawaii, and Australia.

Description: A smallish butterfly, with a wingspan of 25–36mm (1–1$^{1}/_{2}$ inches). The upper surfaces of the wings are dull blue in males, brownish blue in females, with two black spots near the margin of the hindwing, and long slender 'tails' (hence its common name). The undersides are a pale brownish colour, latticed with fine white lines and one broad white streak.

Life-cycle: Varies considerably, according to conditions. Eggs are laid singly on the foodplants, near the flowers. The caterpillars are greenish, pupating before winter and, in Europe, adults may be seen on the wing between May and September, in two to three broods, though elsewhere there may be more. It migrates readily, and individuals have been seen at over 3350m (11,000ft) on Mount Everest.

Larval Foodplants: Various legumes such as gorses (*Ulex* spp.), lupins, bladder senna (*Colutea arborescens*) and others, though in Hawaii it is a pest of broad beans, and elsewhere it may feed on cultivated peas.

General Remarks: A widespread and successful species.

Holly Blue (U.K.) or Spring Azure (U.S.A.)
Celastrina argiolus

Family: Lycaenidae

Habitat: Open woods, parks and gardens.

Distribution: Widespread throughout Europe (except for the extreme north), throughout most of North America and as far south as Panama, in Africa north of the Sahara, and across temperate Asia to the Pacific.

Description: A small butterfly, with a wingspan of only 20–30mm ($^3/_4$–$1^1/_4$ inches). The upper surfaces of the wings are bright blue, edged with black in the male; females have more black colouring, and the second brood is darker than the first. The undersides are greyish-blue, marked with black dots, but without orange (unlike most other blues).

Life-cycle: In much of Europe, this species has an interesting alternating life-cycle. Adults that emerge in spring lay their eggs onto the developing fruits of holly; these eventually emerge as adults in late summer, and the females from this generation lay their eggs onto the developing flowers of ivy. In other areas, this separation of generations is less marked.

Larval Foodplants: Holly (*Ilex aquifolium*), ivy (*Hedera helix*), gorses (*Ulex* spp.), heathers (*Erica* spp.) and others in Europe; dogwoods (*Cornus* spp.), blueberry, and species of *Ceanothus* are used in North America.

General Remarks: Often one of the first butterflies to be seen in spring.

Large Blue *Maculinea arion*

Family: Lycaenidae

Habitat: Rough flowery, sunny locations, especially on hillsides.

Distribution: Widespread, though local in much of Europe, it is absent from the north and the extreme south-west. It became extinct in Britain in 1979 but has since been re-introduced. Also occurs throughout temperate Asia as far east as China.

Description: One of the largest of the blues, though still a relatively small butterfly, with a wingspan of 30–40mm (1¼–1½ inches). The upper surfaces of the wings of both sexes are bright blue, with clear black spots on the forewings. The female is larger than the male, and has a black marginal band on both wings. The under surfaces of the wings are greyish, dusted with blue and dotted with black.

Life-cycle: One of the strangest in the butterfly kingdom. The female lays her eggs onto wild thyme on which at first the caterpillars feed. After a while, they are gathered up by a particular type of ant and taken into their nests. Here, the caterpillars become carnivorous and feed wholly on ant larvae for 10 months, before pupating and eventually crawling out of the nest as adults, quite unmolested by the ants. There is usually one generation, on the wing in June and July.

Larval Foodplants: Wild thyme (*Thymus serpyllum*), followed by ant larvae!

General Remarks: A declining species that has become extinct in many areas. It is now widely protected, and greater understanding of its requirements has increased its chances of survival.

Brown Argus *Aricia agestis*

Family: Lycaenidae

Habitat: Heath and woodland areas and on limestone downs, cliffs and dunes.

Distribution: Occurs throughout Europe except in the northern third, being absent from Scandinavia except in the extreme south. It also occurs across Asia as far east as the Pacific, though there is uncertainty over the exact range due to confusion with similar species.

Description: A small butterfly, with a wingspan of 22–27mm ($^7/_8$–1 inch). It differs from most of its close relatives, the blues, in having no blue colouring, the upper wing surfaces being deep brown, edged with orange spots, while the undersides are greyish-brown with black dots and marginal orange spots.

Life-cycle: The eggs are singly laid on the undersides of leaves. The caterpillars are green with pink stripes, and although they do not have the same complicated relationship with ants as the Large Blue (left), they are tended by ants throughout their life. After pupation in leaf litter, the ants bury the pupae for their own protection. There are two or three generations in a year, depending on the climate, between April and September.

Larval Foodplants: The main foodplant is the rock-rose (*Helianthemun chamaecistus*), though storksbill (*Erodium cicutarium*) and some cranesbills (*Geranium* spp.) are used; Spanish race uses leguminous plants such as bird's foot trefoil (*Lotus corniculatus*).

General Remarks: There is a very closely-related species, the Mountain Argus (*A. artaxerxes*), which differs in minor colour details and in its northern or upland habitat.

Mazarine Blue *Cyaniris semiargus* (pictured left)

Family: Lycaenidae

Habitat: Flowery open hillsides: specially common in mountain areas, though also occurring in lowland areas.

Distribution: Widespread throughout almost the whole of Europe, except for the far north, but absent from Britain where it became extinct in the last century. It also occurs right across the temperate zones of Asia.

Description: A small butterfly with a wingspan of 25–30mm (1–1¼ inches). Not particularly conspicuous, it has plain blue (or purplish-blue) uppersides to all wings, edged with black, and greyish undersides dotted with black. Females are brown above, and similar below, though browner.

Life-cycle: The eggs are laid singly on the upper parts of the foodplant, and the developing caterpillars feed mainly among the flowers and seeds throughout the late summer and autumn. They overwinter as caterpillars, which feed on young leaves in the spring. In mountain areas, there is one generation per year, on the wing from June to August, though in warmer areas there may be two generations.

Larval Foodplants: The flowers and seeds of various leguminous plants, such as clovers (*Trifolium* spp.), bird's foot trefoil (*Lotus corniculatus*) and kidney vetch (*Anthyllis vulneraria*).

General Remarks: May be very abundant in mountain areas, where large numbers (mainly males) gather at puddles and damp patches.

Chalkhill Blue *Lysandra coridon* (pictured left)

Family: Lycaenidae

Habitat: Dry, sunny, grassy locations with abundant flowers, particularly on limestone.

Distribution: Widespread in Europe, though absent from Scandinavia and the far south-west. It barely occurs outside Europe, extending only into Turkey and the western parts of Russia.

Description: A small butterfly, with a wingspan of 30–35mm (1¼–1½ inches). The males are attractive and distinctive with pale silvery-blue uppersides, edged with a black-and-white chequered fringe. The females are brown above, with a similar fringe. Below, the wings are brownish-grey mottled with black, white and orange spots.

Life-cycle: The small white eggs are laid singly on or near the foodplant, and they remain in this state over winter. The growing caterpillars feed mainly at night during the spring, constantly attended by ants which 'milk' them for their sugary secretions, probably protecting them from predators at the same time. There is usually one brood per year, on the wing between June and September, and varying according to locality.

Larval Foodplants: Most frequently on horseshoe vetch (*Hippocrepis comosa*), though may feed on similar related legumes in some areas.

General Remarks: A rather localized species, occurring in separate colonies, though often abundant where it does occur.

Adonis Blue *Lysandra bellargus*

Family: Lycaenidae

Habitat: Dry, sunny and warm open areas with abundant flowers, usually on chalk or limestone.

Distribution: Widespread in the more southerly parts of Europe, but absent from most of Scandinavia. It is confined to the southernmost parts of Britain and also occurs in Asia, as far eastwards as Iran and parts of Russia.

Description: Wingspan 27–32mm (1–1$\frac{1}{4}$ inches). The males are particularly beautiful and conspicuous, the upper surfaces of their wings being a dazzling, almost turquoise blue, edged with a black-and-white chequered fringe. The females are chocolate-brown, sometimes dusted with blue, and the hindwings are edged with a row of orange and black spots. The underwings are greyish-brown, dotted with black, orange and white spots in both sexes.

Life-cycle: The tiny white eggs are laid singly on the leaves of the foodplant. The caterpillars are green and yellow, making them hard to see, even though they often feed during the day. They overwinter as caterpillars, and the first generation of adults appear in May or June, flying until July or August. There is a separate and often more abundant brood from August to September.

Larval Foodplants: Confined to horseshoe vetch (*Hippocrepis comosa*) in Britain, but other similar legumes may be used elsewhere in its range.

General Remarks: This beautiful little insect also has a special relationship with the ants of its habitat, which tend the pupae and caterpillars, guarding them and 'milking' them for sugary liquids.

Common, or Violet Meadow Blue
Polyommatus icarus

Family: Lycaenidae

Habitat: Occurs in a wide variety of habitats, particularly flowery grassland, scrub, open woodland and some types of agricultural land, e.g. fields of lucerne cultivated for cattle fodder.

Distribution: Occurs throughout the whole of Europe, including the far north, also right across temperate Asia (up to 2740m/9000ft in the Himalayas), in northern Africa, and the Canary Isles.

Description: A small butterfly, with a wingspan of 25–30mm ($1-1^{1}/_{4}$ inches). The male butterflies have blue upper surfaces to their wings, edged with a fine line of black and a white (not chequered) fringe; the blue can vary from a pale to an almost violet colour. Females are dark brown above, with orange spots along the edges of the wings. The under surfaces are greyish-brown, marked with black, orange and white spots.

Life-cycle: The small, round white eggs are laid singly on the upper shoots of the foodplants, hatching into greenish caterpillars and the last generation of the year overwinters. In most localities there are two or three generations per year, which tend to overlap, so it can be seen on the wing at almost any time between April and October. The caterpillars are often tended by ants (though not as regularly as with the preceding species), and the pupae may be buried by them.

Larval Foodplants: Various legumes, especially bird's foot trefoil (*Lotus corniculatus*), clovers (*Trifolium* spp.), medicks, and lucerne (*Medicago sativa*).

General Remarks: A common and widespread butterfly, and one of the few blue butterflies to be regularly seen in gardens.

Butterflies

NYMPHALIDAE

Purple Emperor *Apatura iris*

Family: Nymphalidae

Habitat: Mature woodlands and lightly wooded areas bordering water.

Distribution: Occurs widely across the central part of Europe, though is confined to mountain areas further south and is absent from the far north. It also occurs right across temperate Asia as far east as Japan.

Description: A large butterfly, with a wingspan of 55–65mm ($2^{1}/_{4}$–$2^{1}/_{2}$ inches). The males are particularly beautiful, with iridescent purplish-blue upper wing surfaces, streaked with white and edged with brown. The female has similar markings, but lacks the purplish-blue colour. The undersides of the wings are attractively marbled with white, brown, orange and black.

Life-cycle: The eggs are green and spherical, laid singly on the surfaces of leaves. The caterpillars are greyish-brown at first, but become green after hibernation, closely matching the leaves of their foodplant. They are striking creatures, with two horns at the front, though difficult to spot. Adults emerge in June or July, remaining on the wing for one to two months, and there is only one generation.

Larval Foodplants: Sallows and other willows (*Salix* spp.), and occasionally aspens (*Populus tremula*).

General Remarks: Although its foodplants are mainly as above, it has a particular association with large forest trees such as oaks, and can often be seen flying around their upper branches.

White Admiral *Limenitis camilla*

Family: Nymphalidae

Habitat: Woodland in slightly damp locations.

Distribution: Through much of Europe, though absent from extreme southern and northern areas, it is widespread across temperate Asia, including Japan where it is described as a different subspecies.

Description: A medium-sized butterfly with a wingspan of 50–60mm (2–2$\frac{1}{2}$ inches), it is extremely beautiful, with velvety-black wings (soon fading to brown), interrupted by a broad white irregular streak across both wings. The undersides are orange-brown, with a similar white stripe and marginal white patches.

Life-cycle: The tiny spherical, spiny eggs (like miniature sea-urchins) are laid singly on the leaves of the foodplant. On hatching, the caterpillars are brown and spiny, but become green after hibernation, with reddish spines. The pupa is unusually attractive, green and purple with two silvery points. The adults emerge in June or July, flying until August, with just one generation per year.

Larval Foodplants: The only known foodplant is common honeysuckle (*Lonicera periclymenum*) in Europe, and the insects seem to select plants growing in semi-shade.

General Remarks: An active and mobile butterfly with a lovely gliding flight. It settles frequently to feed at such flowers as brambles (*Rubus fruticosus*). The Southern White Admiral (*Limenitis reducta*) replaces this species over much of southern Europe, overlapping in places.

Camberwell Beauty (U.K.), Mourning Cloak (U.S.A.) *Nymphalis antiopa*

Family: Nymphalidae

Habitat: Open woods, scrub, and sheltered grassy locations, though being a highly mobile butterfly it may occur almost anywhere within its range.

Distribution: Widespread around much of the northern hemisphere, it occurs through almost the whole of Europe with the exception of the far south-west and Britain (except as an occasional migrant), across temperate Asia, and throughout the temperate parts of North America.

Description: A large butterfly, with a wingspan of 60–75mm ($2\frac{1}{2}$–3 inches), it is attractively and distinctively marked, with brownish-purple wings edged with blue dots, with a broad yellow margin which fades to white during hibernation. The undersides are a duller version of the upper surfaces, and both sexes are similar.

Life-cycle: The eggs are laid in clusters in early spring, soon hatching into a gregarious mass of black and red spiky caterpillars, feeding in tents of their own making. The adults emerge after pupation in about June and are on the wing until late summer, when they go into hibernation. The overwintered adults are one of the earliest butterflies to be seen in spring, and remain on the wing until about April.

Larval Foodplants: Various deciduous trees, including willows (*Salix* spp.), elms (*Ulmus* spp.), birches (*Betula* spp.), poplars (*Populus* spp.), and hackberry (*Celtis* spp.), often defoliating whole shoots.

General Remarks: The name 'Camberwell Beauty' commemorates the place where it was first found in Britain, in 1748, though it is only a rare visitor.

Peacock *Inachis io*

Family: Nymphalidae

Habitat: Flowery, sunny locations, including grasslands, open woods and gardens.

Distribution: Widespread throughout almost the whole of Europe, except the far north, and across temperate Asia as far as Japan, where there is a separate subspecies.

Description: A large butterfly, with a wingspan of 50–60mm (2–$2\frac{1}{2}$ inches), it has a distinctive pattern on the upper surfaces of the wings, which are reddish-brown with very large multi-coloured eye-spots on each of its four wings – the 'peacock eyes' of its name. The undersides of the wings are uniformly dark brown. Both sexes are similar.

Life-cycle: The eggs are laid in large batches of up to 500 on the undersides of the leaves of the foodplant. The black spiny caterpillars live gregariously – and most conspicuously – in silken webs, reducing the leaves to skeletons as they move across the plant. There is normally one generation per year, the adults emerging in about July, flying until autumn, then overwintering as adults and appearing again in spring.

Larval Foodplants: Most commonly stinging nettles (*Urtica dioica*), less frequently other species of nettle, or hops (*Humulus lupulus*).

General Remarks: A common and popular species, regarded as one of the first harbingers of spring.

Red Admiral *Vanessa atalanta* (pictured left)

Family: Nymphalidae

Habitat: Flowery, sunny places, including gardens. A mobile species that can occur almost anywhere.

Distribution: Widespread, it is found throughout Europe (apart from the extreme north), in north Africa, and across temperate Asia (including northern India). A separate subspecies occurs in the New World, through the United States, Canada and Mexico, and southwards into Central America. It is a mobile migrant, travelling northwards each year in large quantities.

Description: A large butterfly, with a wingspan of 50–60mm (2–2$\frac{1}{2}$ inches). The upper surfaces of the wings are brownish, with a bold red-orange stripe and a wide black-and-white tip on the forewings. The undersides of the forewings are attractively marbled with reddish-orange, blue, white and black. Both sexes are similar.

Life-cycle: The green, barrel-shaped eggs are laid singly on the undersides of leaves. The caterpillars feed singly within a little tent of folded leaves which they construct themselves; they are spiny, and vary in colour from pale brown to greenish-brown. In the more southern parts of the range, the adults hibernate over winter. In northerly parts, including Britain, some attempt to hibernate (but normally fail), while others migrate southwards.

Larval Foodplants: Stinging nettles (*Urtica dioica*), or occasionally hops (*Humulus lupulus*), and other members of the nettle family.

General Remarks: Large numbers gather in autumn to feed at hedgerows and on rotting orchard fruits, such as apples and pears.

Painted Lady *Cynthia cardui* (pictured right)

Family: Nymphalidae

Habitat: A mobile butterfly that can occur in all kinds of sunny, flowery habitats such as gardens, parks, roadsides, meadows and cliff-tops.

Distribution: One of the most widely distributed butterflies in the world, it can be found almost everywhere except for South America and Australasia. Its strongholds are warm temperate zones, such as north Africa and the extreme south of Europe from where it migrates northwards in large numbers. It fails to survive the winter in more extreme climates.

Description: A largish butterfly, with a wingspan of 50–62mm (2–2$\frac{1}{2}$ inches). Within Europe, its wing pattern is distinctive (though there are similar species elsewhere in the world, such as the American Painted Lady). The upper surfaces of the wings are tawny-orange, with black dots and a wide black-and-white tip to the forewings. The undersides of the forewings are similar, while the hindwings are beautifully marbled with brown, cream, grey and blue spots. Both sexes are similar.

Life-cycle: This varies considerably according to locality. In the warmest parts of its range it breeds continuously, so that it is on the wing all year. It migrates to cooler areas where it may breed, but fails to survive the harsher winters. The eggs are laid singly on the foodplant, hatching into caterpillars that usually remain inside a tent of leaves and silk. In Britain, for example, adults can be seen on the wing from April onwards, but only as pale migrants: but from July onwards, numbers are swelled by the more brightly-coloured, home-bred individuals.

Larval Foodplants: Mainly thistles (*Carduus* and *Cirsium* spp.), but also stinging nettles (*Urtica dioica*), and mallows (*Malva* spp.).

General Remarks: Numbers vary greatly in the cooler parts of the range, according to the number of migrants arriving. This depends both on the population in its home range and on the character of the prevailing winds. In Europe, 1996 was an exceptionally good year for the Painted Lady.

Small Tortoiseshell *Aglais urticae* (pictured right)

Family: Nymphalidae

Habitat: Occurs in a wide variety of flowery, sunny locations, including gardens, hedgerows and woodland margins and rides.

Distribution: Throughout Europe and across temperate and subarctic Asia as far as Japan.

Description: A small to medium butterfly, with a wingspan of 40–50mm ($1\frac{1}{2}$–2 inches), the upper surfaces of the wings are reddish-orange, marked with yellow and black patches and a border of blue spots. The undersides are a sombre brown, mottled with yellowish-brown, making the insect quite inconspicuous when at rest. Both sexes are similar.

Life-cycle: The greenish eggs are laid in batches of up to 100 near the top of the foodplant. The black-and-yellow caterpillars feed in groups until fully grown, often reducing the foodplant to a skeleton in the process. When ready to pupate, they separate out, and form into pupae which hang from the foodplant, or other convenient support. There may be two or three generations per year, depending on the temperature, and the last generation of adults hibernate over winter, occasionally appearing on fine days before fully emerging in early spring.

Larval Foodplants: Most frequently stinging nettles (*Urtica dioica*), less commonly *U. urens*.

General Remarks: One of Britain's most familiar butterflies, it is a strong migrant despite its relatively small size.

Comma *Polygonia c-album* (pictured opposite)

Family: Nymphalidae

Habitat: Sheltered, floriferous locations such as gardens, woodland clearings and rides, parks and scrubland. It is a highly mobile butterfly which is likely to appear almost anywhere.

Distribution: Widespread throughout Europe, except for the extreme north, and extending southwards into north Africa and eastwards across temperate Asia as far as Japan; Japanese butterflies are darker and often separated as a subspecies.

Description: A medium-sized butterfly with a wingspan of 44–58mm ($1\frac{3}{4}$–$2\frac{1}{4}$ inches). The upper surfaces of the wings are mottled tawny-orange and black or brown, the most distinctive feature being the strongly indented and convoluted wing margins. With wings folded, the rather dull brownish under surfaces can be seen, together with the feature that gives it both its common and scientific names – a clearly defined white 'c' or comma in the centre of the hindwings.

Life-cycle: The greenish spherical eggs are laid singly or in small groups on the margins of leaves. They hatch into brownish caterpillars with large white marks on their backs, making them look remarkably like bird-droppings and thus enabling them to avoid attracting predators, even when out in the open. In shape, the gold and brown pupae look rather like upside-down sea horses. Adults emerge in the summer, and there is a second brood (or even a third in some places) later, from which the adults hibernate to re-emerge the following spring. Some northwards migration takes place each year into regions where it cannot hope to survive the winter.

Larval Foodplants: Stinging nettles (*Urtica dioica*), elms (*Ulmus* spp.) and hops (*Humulus lupulus*).

General Remarks: The numbers of this species have fluctuated greatly; early in this century, it was one of Britain's rarest butterflies but has gradually expanded and is now generally common over the southern half of Britain.

(*see* p. 47), and is known as *forma prorsa*. The undersides of both forms are similar, with an attractive brown-and-white pattern, rather like a street map. The two generations are so different from one another that they were originally thought to be different species.

Life-cycle: As described above, there are two generations each year. The greenish-white eggs are laid in strings on the foodplant, resembling miniature nettle catkins. These hatch into dark spiky larvae which feed gregariously before pupating on the foodplant. The spring generation flies from April to July, while the autumn generation flies from July to September; occasionally a third brood occurs, intermediate in colouring between the two.

Larval Foodplants: Only stinging nettles (*Urtica dioica*), and related species.

General Remarks: One of relatively few butterflies to have become more common in the last few decades, gradually expanding its range.

Map *Araschnia levana*

Family: Nymphalidae

Habitat: Wooded areas, especially in damper locations and along rivers, mainly lowlands.

Distribution: Occurs mainly in central areas of Europe in a band extending from northern Spain across to Poland, but is largely absent to the north and south of this line. It is seen across temperate Asia as far as Japan, where a separate subspecies occurs.

Description: With a wingspan of 28–40mm (1$\frac{1}{8}$–1$\frac{1}{2}$ inches) and not especially distinctive, this species is one of the more remarkable of European butterflies. The spring generation (known as *forma levana*) resembles a small fritillary, with tawny and black markings on the upper surfaces of the wings. However, the late summer generation looks quite different, resembling a small White Admiral

Silver-Washed Fritillary *Argynnis paphia*

Family: Nymphalidae

Habitat: Woodland, especially where there are glades, and rides with sunshine and flowers.

Distribution: Widespread and generally common in Europe, though absent from northern Scandinavia, the extreme south-west, and northern Britain. It also occurs in north Africa, and across temperate Asia as far as Japan. Several subspecies have been described from different parts of the range.

Description: A large butterfly, with a wingspan of 55–70mm ($2^1/_4$–$2^3/_4$ inches). The upper surfaces of the wings are a beautiful orange-brown, streaked and dotted with black, in a pattern typical of most fritillaries. The undersides of the forewings are similar though paler, but the hindwings – visible at rest – are washed with a silvery-green sheen (the origin of its common name). Although males and females are broadly similar, the females usually have more black on a duller orange background, with slightly different patterning.

Life-cycle: The white conical eggs are laid on the barks of trees, often among moss, and usually about 1–2m (3–6ft) above ground and close to suitable foodplants. The caterpillars overwinter here, without feeding, and descend in the spring in search of their foodplant. The brownish pupae form in June, and are superbly camouflaged among vegetation. Adults emerge in May (or late June in Britain and other cooler regions) and fly until August, with one generation only per year.

Larval Foodplants: Various species of violets (*Viola*).

General Remarks: One of the largest and most distinctive of the fritillaries.

Dark Green Fritillary *Mesoacidalia aglaja*

Family: Nymphalidae

Habitat: Occurs in a variety of unimproved open, flowery locations, such as downland, cliff-tops, grassy sand-dunes, and mountain pastures.

Distribution: Throughout Europe except for a few of the islands, and across temperate Asia as far as Japan.

Description: A medium to large butterfly, with a wingspan of 50–55mm (2–2$\frac{1}{4}$ inches). The upper surfaces of the wings are typical of most fritillaries – tawny orange, with a pattern of dark brown marks and streaks. The under surfaces of the forewings are similar though paler, but the hindwings have a pattern of clear silver spots on a mottled straw-and-green-coloured background. The males and females differ only in small details of colouring and size.

Life-cycle: The yellowish conical eggs are singly laid on the foodplant. The blackish-and-red caterpillars feed little in the autumn and soon go into hibernation, re-emerging in spring to feed voraciously on the growing foodplant. The pupae are brown, suspended among vegetation, and very difficult to detect. Adults emerge in June and fly until about August, in a single generation.

Larval Foodplants: Violets (*Viola* spp.).

General Remarks: A fast-flying species, frequently alighting to feed at flowers.

Queen of Spain Fritillary *Issoria lathonia*

(pictured opposite)

Family: Nymphalidae

Habitat: Open floriferous grassland and scrub, but being a very mobile species it may briefly explore other habitats.

Distribution: Occurs through most of Europe, though only as a migrant in more northerly regions. It also occurs in north Africa, and across temperate Asia as far as China and the Himalayas.

Description: A medium-sized butterfly, with a wingspan of 35–45mm (1$\frac{1}{3}$–1$\frac{3}{4}$ inches). The upper surfaces of the wings bear a resemblance to most other fritillaries – tawny with black markings – though the slightly indented outer margins of the forewings are a useful field identification mark. The under surfaces of the hindwings are boldly marked with large silvery-white blotches in an attractive pattern. There is little difference between male and female.

Life-cycle: The eggs are singly laid on the foodplant and soon hatch into brownish spiky caterpillars. According to the generation and time of year, the caterpillars may feed voraciously or go into hibernation. In favourable warmer localities there may be up to three broods per year, and adults are on the wing from February to October. They are regular and powerful migrants, moving northwards in large numbers in most years. They breed in these northern areas, but are not able to survive the winter.

Larval Foodplants: Mainly violets (*Viola* spp.), but also other low-growing plants.

General Remarks: A fast-flying species that is difficult to approach closely.

Pearl-Bordered Fritillary *Clossiana euphrosyne*

(pictured below)

Family: Nymphalidae

Habitat: Open woodland, forest margins, scrub, damp meadows and heathland.

Distribution: Widely distributed through almost the whole of Europe (with the exception of the far south-west), and across temperate Asia. Scattered throughout Britain, but mainly in the west.

Description: A smallish butterfly with a wingspan of 32–40mm (1¼–1½ inches). The uppersides of the wings are typical of most fritillaries, being mottled black and tawny; the undersides of the hindwings are a mosaic of orange and yellow, with seven silver pearls along the margins and two closer to the body.

Life-cycle: The yellowish eggs are laid singly or in pairs on the leaves of the foodplant. The caterpillars are black with yellowish bristles, and they feed solitarily until pupation after

hibernation. In the northern part of its range there is one generation, with adults flying through May and June, though further south there may be two generations with the second flying until August.

Larval Foodplants: Several species of violets (*Viola*).

General Remarks: An attractive little butterfly, rarely straying far from its hatching site.

Small Pearl-Bordered Fritillary (U.K.), Silver-Bordered Fritillary (U.S.A.) *Clossiana selene*

(pictured below left)

Family: Nymphalidae

Habitat: Woodland margins and clearings, damp meadows, swampy areas, and the edges of heaths, with a tendency to occur on damper sites.

Distribution: Widespread throughout Europe except for the drier, southernmost parts, and across temperate Asia. It is quite common in North America, as several distinct subspecies.

Description: Wingspan 28–38mm (1–1½ inches). The uppersides of the wings are typical of most fritillaries being similar to the Pearl-Bordered Fritillary but with a higher density of dark markings in most forms. The undersides of the hindwings differ from the Pearl-Bordered in having six or seven white patches towards the body, and a stronger ground colour resulting in a more strongly contrasting pattern. It is also a slightly smaller insect.

Life-cycle: Similar to that of the Pearl-Bordered Fritillary, it overwinters in caterpillar form. In northern parts of its range, including Britain, there is only one generation, on the wing between late May and early July (though occasionally there may be a small second generation); further south, there are usually two generations, between May and August.

Larval Foodplants: Violets (*Viola* spp.).

General Remarks: A butterfly that has sadly declined in parts of Europe and North America, due largely to drainage of its habitat.

Glanville Fritillary *Melitaea cinxia*

Family: Nymphalidae

Habitat: Flowery meadows and hillsides. In Britain it is confined to sheltered, floriferous and south-facing coastal undercliffs.

Distribution: Widespread through most of Europe, apart from Mediterranean islands and the extreme north, it is extremely localized in Britain, appearing solely in the Isle of Wight and Channel Islands. It also occurs in north Africa and across much of temperate Asia.

Description: A medium to small butterfly, with a wingspan of 34–40mm ($1\frac{1}{3}$–$1\frac{1}{2}$ inches), the upper surfaces are chequered tawny-orange and black, like most fritillaries. The under surfaces of the hindwings are more distinctive, with three bands of white spots giving a generally paler appearance when it is at rest.

Life-cycle: The yellowish eggs are laid in batches of up to 200 on the leaves of the foodplants. The caterpillars are conspicuous at all stages, feeding and basking gregariously in their silken webs. They are black when young, with reddish heads later on, and they spread out and feed singly after hibernation. In northern parts of the range, including Britain, they have one generation per year, in May to July, though further south there are two broods lasting until September.

Larval Foodplants: Mainly plantains, especially ribwort plantain (*Plantago lanceolata*), though other herbs such as knapweeds (*Centaurea* spp.) may be used.

General Remarks: One of Britain's rarest butterflies, at the north-western edge of its range.

Spotted Fritillary *Melitaea didyma* (pictured right)

Family: Nymphalidae

Habitat: Fields of wild flowers, hillsides and scrub, usually in sunny sheltered sites.

Distribution: Occurs right across southern Europe as far north as northern France and Germany. It also occurs across temperate Asia, and southwards into north Africa, with several subspecies distinguishable in parts of the range.

Description: A smallish butterfly with a wingspan of 30–40mm (1¼–1½ inches). The upper surfaces of the wings are barely distinguishable from other small fritillaries, especially as it is such a variable species. The undersides of the hindwings have three bands of white with black dots and two clear bands of orange.

Life-cycle: The eggs are laid in batches on the leaves of the foodplant, and the caterpillars feed gregariously in silken webs while young, then hibernate in tents of their own making. There may be two or three generations, according to the climate, and in more southerly parts of the range the butterfly is on the wing between May and September.

Larval Foodplants: Various herbaceous plants, but especially plantains (*Plantago* spp.), toadflax (*Linaria vulgaris*), and speedwell (*Veronica chamaedrys*).

General Remarks: There are a number of similar species that are hard to distinguish without close examination.

Heath Fritillary *Mellicta athalia* (pictured below left)

Family: Nymphalidae

Habitat: Woodland margins and rides, flowery fields and moorland – though hardly ever heathland, despite its name.

Distribution: Widespread throughout the whole of Europe, with the exception of the far south-west, and very rare in Britain. It also occurs across temperate Asia as far as Japan, with a number of subspecies distinguishable throughout its range.

Description: With a wingspan of 25–38mm (1–1½ inches) it is a very variable species, being similar in general character to the other small fritillaries, though rather darker, with continuous brown bands around the margins of the wings on the upper surfaces. The undersides are mottled orange and brown with white spots.

Life-cycle: The pale yellowish eggs are laid in batches of up to 150 under a bramble or dead leaf close to the preferred foodplant. The larvae feed gregariously in silken webs, hibernating in small groups under dead leaves. The following spring they spread out and feed less sociably. In northern parts of the range there is just one generation per year, in June to July, but further south there may be two or even three broods between May and August.

Larval Foodplants: Most frequently common cow-wheat (*Melampyrum pratense*), less frequently ribwort plantain (*Plantago lanceolata*), and speedwell (*Veronica chamaedrys*).

General Remarks: Though abundant in mainland Europe, this is one of Britain's rarest butterflies, confined to just a few sites in southern England.

Marsh Fritillary *Eurodryas aurinia*

Family: Nymphalidae

Habitat: Wet meadows, bogs, moorland and floriferous grassland, both wet and dry.

Distribution: Through much of Europe, though absent from large parts of Greece, Italy and northern Scandinavia. It also occurs eastwards across temperate Asia.

Description: A small to medium butterfly, with a wingspan of 30–45mm (1¼–1¾ inches). Although broadly similar in pattern to other small fritillaries, it differs in having many more straw-coloured patches (rather than tawny-orange) on the upper wing surfaces, though it is notoriously variable in its coloration. The underwings are mottled with orange, dull yellow and white, lacking the silvery patches of some species. Females tend to be slightly larger than males.

Life-cycle: The oval, yellowish eggs are laid in large batches on the leaves of the foodplant. The caterpillars are black with white marks, and they live gregariously until winter when they hibernate in silken cocoons among taller vegetation. The following spring they become less sociable, though they are often easy to spot as they make little effort at concealment. Normally, there is just one brood, with the adults emerging in April or May and flying until June or July, depending on the locality.

Larval Foodplants: Most commonly devil's bit scabious (*Succisa pratensis*), but also plantains (*Plantago* spp.) and other herbs, and the Iberian race uses honeysuckles (*Lonicera* spp.).

General Remarks: This species is known to have declined dramatically throughout most of Europe and is now uncommon almost everywhere.

Zebra *Heliconius charitonius* (pictured below)

Family: Nymphalidae

Habitat: Woodlands, especially in and around clearings and margins.

Distribution: Its centre of distribution is tropical America, particularly Central America, but it extends northwards into the United States as far as South Carolina. It is the only species of this tropical genus that breeds in significant numbers in the United States.

Description: A medium to large butterfly, with a wingspan of 75–80mm (3–3¼ inches), but with unusually narrow wings. It is a beautiful and conspicuous butterfly, with black wings boldly striped with yellow, and with a row of yellowish dots on the hindwings.

Life-cycle: The caterpillars are covered with long branching spines and are usually poisonous (according to the plant on which they have been feeding), and will be unappealing to predators as a result. In tropical areas, they are on the wing all year round.

Larval Foodplants: They feed mainly on species of the poisonous passion flower (*Passiflora*).

General Remarks: Most members of this group have numerous mimics, but this species has no close imitators and is easily identified.

Red Lacewing *Cethosia biblis* (pictured above)

Family: Nymphalidae

Habitat: Occurs mainly in wooded areas, particularly in clearings and along forest margins.

Distribution: In the warmer parts of southern Asia, from Pakistan to China, and southwards into Malaysia, the Philippines and adjacent areas.

Description: A large butterfly, with a wingspan of 80–90mm ($3\frac{1}{4}$–$3\frac{1}{2}$ inches). The upper surfaces of the wings are generally orange, varying towards brown or red, with broad black tips, and a series of white 'u' marks in the black borders. The undersides are usually redder, with a band of white, and two zig-zag lines of black and white ending in scalloped borders rather like the edges of lace doyleys.

Life-cycle: Over most of its area it can be seen on the wing at virtually any time of year, with a series of overlapping generations. In the northernmost parts of its range, such as Pakistan, it may disappear for a few months in winter.

Larval Foodplants: Various species of *Passiflora*.

General Remarks: The adults are poisonous or highly distasteful to predators, having absorbed poison from their foodplants during the larval stages.

Flambeau or Orange Flame Butterfly
Dryas julia (pictured right)

Family: Nymphalidae

Habitat: A mobile and wide-ranging species occurring in parks and gardens, along woodland margins, or in clearings.

Distribution: Its main centre of distribution is tropical America, extending northwards into the southern United States, and southwards into South America. It occurs as a breeding species in the southern parts of Texas and Florida, though may occasionally occur further north.

Description: A medium to large butterfly, with a wingspan of 70–90mm ($2\frac{3}{4}$–$3\frac{1}{2}$ inches), and rather narrow wings. It is beautiful and distinctive, due partly to its long narrow shape,

but also to the intense orange colour of the wings. The forewings have black tips and black bands just behind the tips (though these are absent in some subspecies, such as the Jamaican). The hindwings are edged with black.

Life-cycle: The caterpillars, which are heavily armed with long branching spines, feed in loose groups and have a tendency to cannibalism if the food supply runs short. The adults are on the wing virtually all year, except at the edges of their range.

Larval Foodplants: Various species of *Passiflora*.

General Remarks: Where it does occur, this butterfly is often abundant, and can be frequently seen visiting flowers or gathering at wet muddy patches.

Diadem, Six Continent, or Danaid Eggfly Butterfly *Hypolimnas misippus*

Family: Nymphalidae

Habitat: Occurs in a wide range of habitats, including open woodland, parks, gardens and other warm flowery areas.

Distribution: As one of its common names suggests, this is a widespread butterfly (though it does not quite cover six continents). Its main areas of distribution include North America, South America, the West Indies, southern Asia, Australia, and parts of Africa. It is possible that in some parts of its range it was accidentally introduced by early travellers.

Description: A medium to large butterfly, with a wingspan of 60–80mm (2$\frac{1}{3}$–3$\frac{1}{4}$ inches). The males and females are quite different; males are blackish-blue with two blue-edged white spots on each forewing and one larger one on the hindwing. The females mimic the poisonous milkweed butterflies (gaining protection from predators by doing so), and have orange upper surfaces to the wings with broad black tips to the forewings, boldly marked with white. Despite its wide geographical range, there is very little variation in its appearance wherever it occurs.

Life-cycle: The caterpillars are densely covered in fine spines, feeding in loose groups on the foodplant. The Diadem is continuously on the wing for most of the year, though it tends to be most abundant during rainy seasons.

Larval Foodplants: Various species of purslane (*Portulaca*) and its close relatives.

General Remarks: The males are usually highly territorial, taking up prominent positions and defending a territory by driving away other male intruders of their own or different species.

Owl Butterfly *Caligo eurilochus*

Family: Nymphalidae

Habitat: Occurs around woodland areas, and in plantations, parks and well-wooded gardens.

Distribution: The warmer parts of South America, as far south as Argentina.

Description: A large butterfly with a wingspan of 130–140mm (5–5$\frac{1}{2}$ inches), and very broad wings. Overall, it is marbled brown with paler patches and small white areas. The forewings have a broad, pale orange margin, and there is a large dark white-edged eye-spot on each hindwing, giving rise to the common name 'owl' butterfly. These large eye-spots may well frighten potential predators into thinking that they are dealing with a much more substantial prey.

Life-cycle: On the wing for most of the year in tropical areas, and, unlike most butterflies (which are sun-loving), they emerge mainly at dusk and dawn, presumably to avoid predation, further living up to their name.

Larval Foodplants: Members of the species *Musa*, including cultivated bananas, though they rarely occur in sufficient numbers to be pests.

General Remarks: Despite their large size, these butterflies are surprisingly difficult to spot, thanks to their cryptic coloration and habit of avoiding daylight.

Tree Nymph *Idea leuconoe*

Family: Nymphalidae

Habitat: Occurs mainly in heavily forested areas, where its pale, slightly ghostly appearance has given rise to various local legends.

Distribution: A south-east Asian species, distributed across parts of China, Japan, Malaya, Java, Borneo and the Philippines.

Description: A large butterfly, with a wingspan of 95–110mm ($3^{3}/_{4}$–$4^{1}/_{3}$ inches). When newly emerged, it has a strikingly conspicuous pattern of black markings on a white background, edged with black dotted with white. As it ages, the white becomes yellower and the black becomes greyer, making it appear even more spectral in its dimly-lit forest environment.

Life-cycle: In most parts of its range the species is on the wing all year, tending to be more active in the evenings. It has a slow fluttering flight, with heavy wing-beats interspersed with periods of gliding.

Larval Foodplants: Various native forest shrubs such as the species *Parsonsia* and *Tylophora*.

General Remarks: A striking species, often seen in butterfly houses in many parts of the world, as it is relatively easy to rear and keep. There are several closely-related species including *I. idea* which is one of the largest species of butterflies anywhere.

Garden Acraea *Acraea horta*

Family: Nymphalidae

Habitat: Occurs in a variety of open floriferous and semi-shaded habitats, such as parks and gardens, open forests and savannah.

Distribution: Widespread in southern Africa.

Description: A medium-sized butterfly, with a wingspan of 44–55mm ($1^{3}/_{4}$–$2^{1}/_{4}$ inches). The males are a reddish-orange in colour and have transparent forewing tips, the hindwings being heavily spotted with black, especially close to the body; the undersides are similar though paler. Females are broadly similar, but generally paler, and with a pronounced chequered border to the hindwings.

Life-cycle: The eggs are laid in batches on the foodplants and, initially, the young caterpillars feed together. They are covered with branched hairs which afford protection from predators. In warmer parts of the range the butterflies are on the wing continuously throughout the year, but in cooler southern parts they are present as adults in summer only. At times, there are mass emergences, and large numbers may be seen together.

Larval Foodplants: Various passion flowers (*Passiflora* spp.) may be used, as well as the South African wild peach (*Kiggelaria africana*).

General Remarks: An attractive, slow-flying butterfly that keeps close to the ground. There are several similar species in South Africa.

White-barred Charaxes *Charaxes brutus*

Family: Nymphalidae

Habitat: Occurs mainly in forest and thick bush, less frequently in more open habitats.

Distribution: In the southern parts of Africa, including South Africa, Zimbabwe and parts of Mozambique and Botswana.

Description: Large, with a wingspan of 70–100mm ($2^{3}/_{4}$–4 inches), they are beautiful insects, with black wings boldly marked with broad white stripes that begin on the forewings as a row of dots, coalescing and widening through the hindwings which have two tails of roughly the same length. The undersides are quite different, with a reddish-brown ground colour dotted with black, white and blue, and a similar white band. Males and females are alike.

Life-cycle: The caterpillars feed singly and are most distinctive due to the antler-like projections on their heads. The adults are on the wing all year in warmer parts of the range, and are most common in summer and autumn.

Larval Foodplants: Various trees and shrubs, particularly Natal mahogany, forest mahogany, wild honeysuckle tree and Cape ash.

General Remarks: Powerful and fast-flying, both males and females feed on fermenting fruit or similar nutrient-rich damp materials, and may occasionally gather at mud-holes. The males are distinctly territorial.

Cape Autumn Widow or Autumn Brown
Dira clytus

Family: Nymphalidae

Habitat: Occurs mainly in open grassy areas where there are abundant flowers, especially on lower mountain slopes.

Distribution: Widespread in southern South Africa, particularly around Cape Province.

Description: A medium-sized butterfly, with a wingspan of 50–58mm (2–2$\frac{1}{4}$ inches). The forewings are dark brown with a scattering of white spots towards the tips where there are double, blue-centred eye-spots. The hindwings are dark brown, with ill-defined eye-spots and the undersides are similar in pattern, with less white. Males and females are very similar in appearance.

Life-cycle: The eggs are laid singly and soon hatch out into greenish caterpillars. These are largely nocturnal, spending the day hidden at the bases of clumps of grass. There is only one generation of adults each year, on the wing in late summer from March to May.

Larval Foodplants: Various species of tussocky grasses.

General Remarks: This species is often abundant where it does occur and can be seen on the wing in dull weather, or even light rain.

Gold-Banded Forester *Euphaedra neophron*

Family: Nymphalidae

Habitat: Warm subtropical forest areas, particularly around clearings and margins.

Distribution: Warmer subtropical areas of southern Africa, including parts of South Africa, Zimbabwe and Mozambique.

Description: A medium to large butterfly with a wingspan of 65–75mm (2½–3 inches), the female being generally larger than the male. They are attractive creatures, with electric- or metallic-blue wings, heavily marked on the forewings with gold bands edged with black. The undersides are much paler and provide more camouflage, being mottled with a pinkish-brown pattern.

Life-cycle: The larvae feed singly, and are particularly distinctive by virtue of their long feathery projections, which serve to break up their outlines, making them less conspicuous. The adults are on the wing all year.

Larval Foodplants: The sole larval foodplant appears to be the forest undershrub, the dune soap-berry (*Deinbollia oblongifolia*).

General Remarks: Fast-flying and conspicuous butterflies that frequently bask in the sun or visit mud-patches; however, they quickly disappear into the shadow of the forest if disturbed.

Yellow Pansy *Junonia hierta* (pictured right)

Family: Nymphalidae

Habitat: Commonly seen in a wide variety of sunny and open areas of grassland and savannah.

Distribution: Widespread through most of southern Africa, apart from parts of the Cape Province.

Description: A medium-sized butterfly, with a wingspan of 45–50mm (1¾–2 inches). The males are beautiful and have blackish wings, each with large gold-edged yellowish patches, bright blue patches at the junction of the forewings and hindwings, and white patches at the tips of each forewing. The undersides are a much paler greyish-brown. Females are less boldly marked, with fewer orange markings and smaller purplish spots in place of the blue.

Life-cycle: The yellowish eggs are singly laid and hatch into spiny brownish caterpillars. In warmer parts of the range, the butterflies are on the wing all year, while in cooler areas they can be seen from August to May.

Larval Foodplants: The larvae feed on a wide variety of herbaceous plants from many different families, including *Adhatoda densiflora*, *Barleria pungens* and others.

General Remarks: A common species that regularly visits gardens. The males are territorial, taking up defensible perches on bare ground. When disturbed, they immediately close their wings, revealing the more cryptic coloration of their underwings.

Life-cycle: Because of the wide range of climatic conditions experienced by this species, its life-cycle varies considerably. In southern, warmer, areas it may have three broods throughout the summer, though further north, or in the mountains, there may be just a single brood, in midsummer.

Larval Foodplants: The larvae feed on various wild and cultivated cherries, willows (*Salix* spp.), poplars (*Populus* spp.), plums (*Prunus* spp.) and apples (*Malus* spp.), though rarely become pests.

General Remarks: There are several subspecies throughout the range, and a number of closely-related species within the western United States.

Lorquin's Admiral
Basilarchia (Limenitis) lorquini (pictured right)

Family: Nymphalidae

Habitat: Occurs in a wide variety of open and semi-shaded habitats, such as forest margins and glades, parks, gardens, orchards and shelter-belts.

Distribution: Widespread in the west of North America, from British Columbia southwards to Baja California.

Description: A medium-sized butterfly, with a wingspan of 50–65mm (2–2½ inches). The upper sides of the wings are dark blackish-brown, shading to orange-brown towards the tips. Across both wings there are bold interrupted white bands, with smaller areas of white on either side. The undersides are paler, echoing the same pattern.

Butterflies

SATYRIDAE

Marbled White *Melanargia galathea*

Family: Satyridae

Habitat: Rough, sunny, flowery locations, with long grasses.

Distribution: Widespread throughout the southern part of Europe and northwards as far as northern Germany and southern Britain. It also occurs in north Africa and western temperate Asia.

Description: A medium-sized butterfly with a wingspan of 45–55mm (1$\frac{3}{4}$–2$\frac{1}{4}$ inches), its name describes it accurately, the upper surfaces of the wings being beautifully and conspicuously marbled with black on white. The undersides are similar, but paler and more yellowish, with clusters of eye-spots. Males and females are very similar except for slight colour differences.

Life-cycle: The eggs are scattered over rough grassy areas and are therefore virtually impossible to detect. Soon after hatching, the young caterpillar goes into hibernation, re-emerging in spring to feed on its foodplant by night. Adults emerge after pupation in June and are on the wing until August, with just one short generation per year.

Larval Foodplants: Various grasses, of which the fescues (*Festuca* spp.) are the most important, though coarser species such as cock's foot (*Dactylis glomerata*) and tor grass (*Brachypodium pinnatum*) may be used.

General Remarks: In favoured sites this butterfly may be extremely abundant, and it is one of the finest sights of high summer to see thousands of these beautiful insects dancing over rough flowery grassland.

Woodland Grayling *Hipparchia fagi*

Family: Satyridae

Habitat: Open woodland or scrub with trees, in warm sheltered areas.

Distribution: Occurs in a band across the central part of Europe, from the mountains of northern Spain, eastwards through France, Italy and the Balkans, and into the western parts of Russia.

Description: One of the larger graylings, with a wingspan of 60–70mm ($2^{1}/_{2}$–$2^{3}/_{4}$ inches). The upper surfaces of the wings are dark brown with a broad pale band towards the outer edges, and an eye-spot at the tip of each forewing. Females are rather more boldly coloured than the males. The undersides of the wings are similar to the upper surfaces, though slightly paler.

Life-cycle: The eggs are laid singly among grasses. The caterpillars feed for a while in autumn, then hibernate, re-emerging in spring to feed until early summer when they pupate. The adults emerge in June and fly until about August, with just one generation per year.

Larval Foodplants: Various grasses, especially of the genus *Holcus*, such as creeping soft-grass.

General Remarks: The butterflies frequently perch on trees with their wings closed and because of the cryptic coloration of the undersides of the wings are very hard to spot.

Grayling *Hipparchia semele*

Family: Satyridae

Habitat: Rough, dry floriferous locations such as cliff-tops, heaths, dry stony hillsides and steppe.

Distribution: Widespread through almost the whole of Europe apart from northern Scandinavia; in Britain it is mainly coastal, being concentrated in the south. It also extends eastwards across Russia.

Description: A medium-sized butterfly, with a wingspan of 50–55mm (2–2$\frac{1}{4}$ inches). The upper surfaces of the wings are brown with a broad irregular paler band of orange or yellowish-brown, punctuated by two eye-spots on the forewing and one on the hindwing. The undersides are rather similar, except for the hindwings, which have a marbled greyish-brown pattern that provides perfect camouflage when the butterfly is at rest with its wings closed. Males and females differ only in small details. Southern European individuals tend to be much larger than those from north-west Europe.

Life-cycle: The spherical white eggs are laid singly on grasses. They hatch into brownish striped caterpillars which feed for a while before hibernating. These re-emerge and feed throughout the spring, mainly at night, before pupating. The adults emerge in June in the south of the range, or July further north, flying until August or September, with only one generation per year.

Larval Foodplants: Various grasses, especially the finer ones such as fescues (*Festuca* spp.), or marram grass (*Ammophila arenaria*).

General Remarks: Graylings spend little time flying, most of their time being spent perched on the ground or on low vegetation. When at rest, they immediately close their wings, and angle themselves towards the sun so that they cast no shadow. As a result of their cryptic coloration they can be very hard to see until disturbed.

Great Banded Grayling *Brintesia circe*

(pictured above)

Family: Satyridae

Habitat: Scrub, light woodland and sunny, grassy places with scattered trees or rocks.

Distribution: A local species with a scattered distribution across the warmer parts of Europe, especially Spain, France and Italy, extending eastwards through southern temperate Asia to the Himalayas.

Description: Similar to the Woodland Grayling (p. 73) in size and markings, though the band of colour across the wings is much clearer and almost white, with a single large spot on the forewing. The undersides of the wings have an additional band of white, and the overall effect in flight is of a white striped butterfly. Males and females are very similar.

Life-cycle: The eggs are laid singly among grasses and soon hatch out into caterpillars which feed for a while, then hibernate. The striped caterpillars re-emerge in spring and feed until May or June, when they pupate. The adults emerge in June and fly until August, in a single generation per year.

Larval Foodplants: Various taller grasses, such as wood false brome (*Brachypodium sylvaticum*).

General Remarks: A beautiful and conspicuous butterfly that flies readily and settles frequently on rocks, trees and even roadways. It may be abundant in favoured localities.

Scotch Argus *Erebia aethiops* (pictured right)

Family: Satyridae

Habitat: Damp grassy areas, particularly in uplands, and often close to woodland, though in a few areas it occurs at sea-level on sand-dunes.

Distribution: Scattered through the hillier parts of Europe, though absent from both the far north and extreme south, it extends eastwards into the western parts of Russia.

Description: A small to medium butterfly with a wingspan of 35–40mm ($1^{1}/_{3}$–$1^{1}/_{2}$ inches). The upper surfaces of the wings are velvety-brown with rust-coloured bands punctuated by eye-spots. The undersides of the forewings are similar, though the hindwings are duller. In general, males are smaller and darker than females, though this is a very variable species over its entire range.

Life-cycle: The yellowish eggs are singly laid, deep in tussocks of grass on which the caterpillars feed. They feed for a while, then hibernate, emerging in the spring to continue feeding until about June, when they pupate. Adults first appear in June and fly until August, with only one generation per year, as with most mountain species of butterfly.

Larval Foodplants: Tussocky grasses, such as blue moor grass (*Sesleria caerulea*) on limestone, or purple moor grass (*Molinia caerulea*) in more acid sites.

General Remarks: An uncommon butterfly overall, it is protected in several countries and the species may be very abundant where it does occur. In sunny weather, hundreds of insects can be seen slowly flying over rough grassland.

Meadow Brown *Maniola jurtina*

Family: Satyridae

Habitat: In the north of the range it occurs in a wide variety of open grassy locations, including agriculturally-improved grasslands. Further south, it can be seen in open grassy woodlands.

Distribution: Widespread throughout Europe except for the far northern parts of Scandinavia. It also occurs eastwards through Asia as far as Iran, and southwards into north Africa.

Description: A medium-sized butterfly with a wingspan of 45–50mm ($1\frac{1}{2}$–$2\frac{1}{4}$ inches). The males are a dull brown with a poorly-defined band of orange on the forewing, and a single eye-spot towards the tip of the forewing. This eye-spot normally has just one white dot in its centre (except in one form of the Meadow Brown), unlike the Gatekeeper (p. 78), which always has two white spots. Females are rather similar, but the orange patches and the eye-spots are brighter and more obvious. The undersides of the hindwings, often the only parts visible when at rest, are dull brown to greyish.

Life-cycle: The eggs are laid singly or dropped among grasses. The caterpillar hatches in late summer, feeds for a while, then goes into hibernation. It re-emerges in spring, feeding mostly at night, and eventually turning bright green. The adults first appear in June and fly until September, normally in just one generation, though there may sometimes be a second one.

Larval Foodplants: Various grasses, but especially the meadow-grasses (*Poa* spp.), and other medium–fine species.

General Remarks: One of the most abundant butterflies in Europe, with huge numbers occurring in most years in a wide variety of grassy habitats.

Ringlet *Aphantopus hyperantus*

Family: Satyridae

Habitat: Grassy places along hedgerows and forest margins, or among scrub, usually at the damper end of such habitats.

Distribution: Widespread and frequently seen throughout most of Europe, though absent from the far south and arctic areas. Also occurs eastwards across temperate parts of Asia.

Description: A small to medium butterfly with a wingspan of 38–46mm ($1^{1}/_{2}$–$1^{3}/_{4}$ inches). It is an inconspicuous though rather attractive butterfly, with dark velvety-brown upper surfaces to the wings and inconspicuous eye-spots with white fringes. The undersides, frequently visible at rest, are more distinctive, with five bright eye-spots on the hindwing, and two or three on the forewing, on a paler brown background.

Life-cycle: The pale yellowish eggs are dropped singly and apparently at random among suitable grasses. The young caterpillars pass the winter in the bases of the grass clumps, re-emerging to feed in the following spring. The full-grown caterpillars are yellowish-brown, and feed nocturnally. After pupation, adults appear in June or July, remaining on the wing throughout the summer (though in Britain and some other northern areas, their life-span is no more than a month). There is only one generation per year.

Larval Foodplants: Coarse tufted grasses, including cock's foot (*Dactylis glomerata*) and couch grass (*Agropyron repens*).

General Remarks: A widespread and often abundant butterfly, though rarely noticed by the general public. Adults are particularly fond of visiting the flowers of bramble (*Rubus fruticosus*).

Gatekeeper or Hedge Brown *Pyronia tithonus*

Family: Satyridae

Habitat: Hedgerows, woodland rides and margins, and scrub.

Distribution: Throughout the southern parts of Europe, apart from the extreme south-east, but absent from Scandinavia and north-east Europe; common in southern Britain. It also occurs in Turkey, but no further east.

Description: A small to medium butterfly with a wingspan of 40–47mm ($1\frac{1}{2}$–$1\frac{7}{8}$ inches), it resembles the Meadow Brown (p. 76), but with a rather more clearly-marked orange band on the upper surfaces of the wings, and an eye-spot containing two white dots. The undersides of the hindwings are marbled brown and cream, with a cluster of eye-spots. Females are distinctly bigger than males.

Life-cycle: The straw-coloured eggs are singly laid on or close to grasses in sheltered places. The caterpillars hibernate while still small, re-emerging in spring in a dull brownish or greenish form that feed mainly at night. They pupate in June, and adults emerge in late June or July, flying until August or September in a single annual generation.

Larval Foodplants: Various fine to medium grasses, such as bents (*Agrostis* spp.), fescues (*Festuca* spp.), and the meadow grasses (*Poa* spp.).

General Remarks: The adult butterflies rarely fly far and regularly alight on flowers such as bramble (*Rubus fruticosus*), ragwort (*Senecio jacobaea*), or marjoram (*Origanum vulgare*), to gather nectar.

Large Heath (U.K.) or Ringlet (U.S.A.)
Coenonympha tullia (pictured right)

Family: Satyridae

Habitat: Bogs, moors and other damp, usually acidic, locations.

Distribution: Scattered through central and northern Europe, from Britain and eastern France eastwards, though absent from the extreme north. It also occurs across temperate Asia. In North America it occurs widely, especially in mountain areas where there are bogs and wet meadows.

Description: A small to medium butterfly, with a wingspan of 36–41mm ($1^{3}/_{8}$–$1^{5}/_{8}$ inches). The upper surfaces of the wings are a dull brownish-orange, though they are rarely seen since the insect rests with wings closed. The undersides are a more distinctive greyish-brown with a broad irregular white streak and various amounts of white-ringed eye-spots. It is a variable species with a number of recognized races or subspecies.

Life-cycle: The large pale eggs are laid singly onto the foodplant. The young caterpillar hibernates, then re-emerges and feeds by day and night throughout the spring. It pupates in May to June, and the single generation of adults emerge in June, flying until August. In North America there are varying numbers of broods, from several in western areas to just one in the far north and high Rockies.

Larval Foodplants: Various sedges and grasses, especially types of cotton grass (*Eriophorum* spp.), and white-beaked sedge (*Rhynchospora alba*).

General Remarks: The adult butterflies are rarely seen visiting flowers.

Small Heath *Coenonympha pamphilus*
(pictured below left)

Family: Satyridae

Habitat: Rough grassy locations of various kinds.

Distribution: Very widespread in Europe, occurring through almost the whole of the continent, except for the far north. It also occurs in north Africa, parts of the Middle East, and temperate western Asia.

Description: A smallish butterfly with a wingspan of 23–33mm (1–$1^{1}/_{3}$ inches), the Small Heath is closely related to the Large Heath and looks quite similar, though smaller. The upper surfaces differ in having one or two eye-spots, and so do the undersides, being less boldly marked with an ill-defined yellowish band and more inconspicuous eye-spots.

Life-cycle: The yellowish-brown eggs are singly laid on or among grasses and the caterpillars from the last generation of the year overwinter, like those of many species in this family, re-emerging in spring to feed quite openly by day on grasses. After pupation, the first generation of adults emerge in April or May, to be followed by one or two more broods, according to weather conditions.

Larval Foodplants: Various fine to medium grasses, such as bents (*Agrostis* spp.) or fescues (*Festuca* spp.).

General Remarks: A common and widespread butterfly that is able to survive and flourish in a wide range of grassy habitats.

Speckled Wood *Pararge aegeria*

Family: Satyridae

Habitat: Woodland rides, clearings and edges, or other shady habitats. This species can tolerate more shade than most butterflies.

Distribution: Widespread through virtually the whole of Europe, except for the far north, it also occurs in north Africa and the western parts of Asia.

Description: A medium-sized butterfly, with a wingspan of 40–45mm ($1^{1}/_{2}$–$1^{3}/_{4}$ inches). The upper surfaces of the wings are attractively chequered with brown and cream, with three or four eye-spots on the hindwings, and one on each forewing. The southern race, which occurs throughout southern Europe, is of a more orange colour, resembling a Wall Brown (opposite), though with more brown on the wings, and scalloped wing margins. The undersides of the forewings resemble the upper surfaces, though the hindwings are somewhat duller, lacking the cream or orange patches.

Life-cycle: The eggs are singly laid on grasses, usually in semi-shade and the insect may then hibernate either in caterpillar or pupal form, which leads to a complicated series of overlapping generations. It may have anything between one and three generations, depending on climate, and is on the wing for much of the period between March and October.

Larval Foodplants: Various coarser grasses, such as cock's foot (*Dactylis glomerata*), and couch grass (*Agropyron repens*).

General Remarks: An attractive and distinctive butterfly, nearly always to be found in shaded or partly-shaded areas. The adults rarely visit flowers, preferring to feed on honeydew.

Wall Brown *Lasiommata megera*

Family: Satyridae

Habitat: Rough grassy areas, especially where there are patches of warm bare ground. Old quarries and cliff-tops or undercliffs are particularly favoured.

Distribution: This species occurs through almost the same European range as the Speckled Wood, though it only just extends into southern Scandinavia. It ranges into north Africa, and eastwards into Asia.

Description: Wingspan 38–48mm ($1^1/_2$–$1^7/_8$ inches). The upper wing surfaces are attractively marbled with orange and brown, rather like a fritillary, though they also have single large eye-spots on the forewings and several smaller ones on the hindwings. The undersides of the forewings are similar to the upper surfaces, but the hindwing undersides are a much duller greyish-brown.

Life-cycle: The eggs are laid singly or in small batches on the leaves or roots of the foodplants, often around an area of bare ground. The caterpillars from the last generation of the year hibernate, then re-emerge to feed mainly at night, through until March or April. The first generation of adults appear soon afterwards, and there may be two or three generations throughout the summer. In warm localities, the butterfly can be seen at virtually any time between April and October.

Larval Foodplants: Various coarser grasses such as cock's foot (*Dactylis glomerata*), Yorkshire fog (*Holcus lanatus*), and wavy hair-grass (*Deschampsia flexuosa*).

General Remarks: These are sun-loving butterflies, living in small colonies in warm areas and frequently alighting on patches of bare ground to bask with their wings almost fully open.

Butterflies

DANAIDAE

Monarch, Wanderer, or Milkweed Butterfly
Danaus plexippus (pictured left)

Family: Danaidae

Habitat: Areas of abundant flowers. A very mobile butterfly that may occur almost anywhere within its range.

Distribution: Widespread throughout North, Central and South America, south-east Asia, Australia, New Zealand, and the Canary Islands, with migrants appearing elsewhere.

Description: A large butterfly, with a wingspan of 75–100mm (3–4 inches). The upper surfaces of the wings are bright orange, veined with black and tipped with an area of black dotted with white. The margins of both wings are black dotted with white. The undersides are similar, but slightly paler.

Life-cycle: The number and timing of the broods of this butterfly vary enormously according to its location. In cooler areas, such as North America, it migrates northwards during spring and early summer, breeds, then migrates southwards in autumn to huge communal roosts in Mexico and elsewhere. In the warmest areas, it may produce continuous broods.

Larval Foodplants: The most common larval foodplants are the various milkweeds (*Asclepia* spp.). These are poisonous, and the toxins are stored by the caterpillar before being passed on to the butterfly which makes it highly unpalatable to predators. Other foodplants are sometimes used, and the butterflies raised on non-toxic plants are themselves non-poisonous.

General Remarks: One of the most successful and interesting of the world's butterflies, with spectacular habits of migration and hibernation.

Plain Tiger, African Monarch or Lesser Wanderer *Danaus chrysippus* (pictured left)

Family: Danaidae

Habitat: Flowery locations. A mobile, free-ranging butterfly.

Distribution: A widespread species, occurring throughout Africa, the Middle East, across Asia, and in Australia and Fiji.

Description: A medium to large butterfly, with a wingspan of 66–82mm ($2\frac{1}{2}$–$3\frac{1}{4}$ inches). It resembles the Monarch, but is smaller, with less defined black veins, and rather more white within the black wingtips.

Life-cycle: The caterpillars are beautifully marked with black, yellow and pale blue and because they occur in so many places, with very different climates, the life-cycles of the butterflies vary enormously. In cooler temperate areas, such as Japan or South Australia, there are one or two generations per year, while in tropical areas there may be up to 12 generations, allowing the butterflies to be on the wing all year.

Larval Foodplants: Most frequently recorded are the milkweeds (*Asclepia* spp.), though unrelated plants are occasionally used.

General Remarks: There are many mimics of the species, possibly taking advantage of the fact that predators mostly avoid it.

Queen Butterfly *Danaus gilippus*

Family: Danaidae

Habitat: Various flowery places.

Distribution: The southern United States, Mexico, the Caribbean islands, and South America. A non-migratory species, unlike the Monarch, with its own local subspecies.

Description: A medium to large butterfly with a wingspan of 70–75mm (2 ³/₄–3 inches), it is similar in general coloration to the Monarch and Plain Tiger butterflies, but has a much smaller black wingtip, and a series of white dots right across the forewing.

Life-cycle: There are one to two generations per year, according to climate. The males are unusual in having a pair of special hair-thin glands which disperse scent during mating. These attract only females of the same species and are thought to be an important means of differentiating them from their mimics.

Larval Foodplants: Mainly milkweeds (*Asclepia* spp.), though other species may also be used.

General Remarks: There are several mimics of this species which take advantage of the fact that predators are likely to avoid it due to its poisonous nature and warning colours.

Butterflies

HESPERIIDAE

Grizzled Skipper *Pyrgus malvae*

Family: Hesperiidae

Habitat: Flowery grassland and other open, sunny sites.

Distribution: Widespread through much of Europe, though absent from the northern parts of Scandinavia and Britain. It also occurs, in several different subspecies, across the temperate parts of Asia.

Description: A very small butterfly with a wingspan of 22–25mm (³⁄₄–1 inch). The upper surfaces of the wings are conspicuously chequered with white and dark brown, and the margins have a distinctive black and white fringe. The under surfaces are similar, though paler and with more brown.

Life-cycle: The yellowish eggs are singly laid, soon hatching into yellow-green caterpillars which feed within loose tents of leaves and silken threads. They overwinter in pupal form. In cooler areas, including Britain, there is normally only one brood per year, in May or June. Further south, there may be two broods, lasting until August.

Larval Foodplants: A wide range of foodplants are used, mainly of the rose family, including wild strawberry (*Fragaria vesca*), tormentil (*Potentilla erecta*), agrimony (*Agrimonia eupatoria*), blackberry (*Rubus fruticosus*) and mallows (*Malva* spp).

General Remarks: An attractive little butterfly, fond of darting to and fro before settling on warm patches of ground, where its chequered pattern may make it difficult to see.

Chequered Skipper (U.K.), Arctic Skipper (U.S.A.) *Carterocephalus palaemon*

Family: Hesperiidae

Habitat: Woodland clearings and sheltered sunny grassy places.

Distribution: Widespread in Europe, though local and absent from the far north and far south. It is widespread in the northern parts of North America and throughout temperate Asia, including Japan.

Description: A small butterfly, with a wingspan of 20–30mm ($^3/_4$–$1^1/_4$ inches). The upper surfaces of the wings are attractively chequered with pale yellow on dark brown; the under surfaces are similar, with a network of black lines.

Life-cycle: The eggs are laid singly, then hatch within a month; most of the rest of the year, including the winter, is spent as a steadily-growing caterpillar. The adults appear in mid-May and fly until June or July, in a single generation.

Larval Foodplants: Various grasses, including purple moor grass (*Molinia caerulea*), and wood false brome (*Brachypodium sylvaticum*).

General Remarks: This butterfly lives in small, often isolated colonies, and can easily go unnoticed, especially if the weather is poor during its flight period. In Britain, its English colonies became extinct about 30 years ago, and it now only occurs in Scotland. In North America, the Checkered Skipper is actually a different species, *Pyrgus communis*.

Dingy Skipper *Erynnis tages* (pictured below)

Family: Hesperiidae

Habitat: Warm, sheltered floriferous grassland, especially on limestone.

Distribution: Throughout Europe, except for northern Scandinavia and the far north of Britain, occurring in mountain areas up to at least 2000m (6600ft).

Description: A very small butterfly, with a wingspan of 25–30mm (1–1¼ inches). Its appearance lives up to its common name – dingy – in the sense that the upper wing surfaces are a dull brown, only faintly marked with small pale dots so that it bears more resemblance to a moth than a butterfly. The under surfaces of the wings are orange-brown, lightly marked with white.

Life-cycle: The pale orange eggs are laid singly on the foodplant, hatching in 4-6 weeks into greenish caterpillars which feed in loose tents which they spin around themselves and the leaves of the foodplant. The caterpillar overwinters, pupating in the following spring. In cooler areas there is only one generation, with the butterflies on the wing between May and July, though further south there are two generations, on the wing from May to August.

Larval Foodplants: Bird's foot trefoil (*Lotus corniculatus*), horseshoe vetch (*Hippocrepis comosa*), and some members of the carrot family such as the sea holly (*Eryngium maritimum*).

General Remarks: This little butterfly is dependent on the sun for activity; in dull weather it rests on vegetation or bare earth, merging inconspicuously into the background.

Small Skipper *Thymelicus sylvestris* (pictured right)

Family: Hesperiidae

Habitat: Rough grassy locations, especially where there are abundant flowers.

Distribution: Widespread throughout almost the whole of Europe, except for most of Scandinavia and northern Britain. Abundant in southern Europe, it also occurs in western Asia.

Description: A small butterfly, with a wingspan of 28–30mm (1–1¼ inches). The upper surfaces of the wings are orange-brown, darkening towards the edges; males have a single dark line across the centre – the scent brand. The under surfaces are paler, without the dark edges. The antennae have orange clubs which are tipped with black only on the upper surfaces (*see* Essex Skipper p. 90).

Life-cycle: The eggs are laid in rows on the leaf-sheaths of the foodplants. They hatch in late summer when the young caterpillars immediately go into hibernation without feeding. The following spring they feed avidly until late May when they pupate, the adults emerging in June. There is a single generation, on the wing from May or June until August.

Larval Foodplants: A variety of larger grasses, such as Yorkshire fog (*Holcus lanatus*) and timothy (*Phleum pratense*).

General Remarks: Small Skippers are one of a small group of butterflies which rest with their wings held angled up, only half open.

Essex Skipper (U.K.), European Skipper (U.S.A.) *Thymelicus lineola*

Family: Hesperiidae

Habitat: Flowery, grassy places; common in hay meadows in northern North America.

Distribution: Widespread throughout most of Europe, with the exception of northern Scandinavia and the northern part of Britain. It was introduced into Canada early this century and has steadily extended its range into the United States. It also occurs across temperate Asia.

Description: A small butterfly, with a wingspan of 19–31mm ($^3/_4$–$1^1/_4$ inches). It is very similar in size, shape and colouring to the Small Skipper (p. 88), differing in its slightly paler colour, and the fact that the antennae are tipped all round with black, as if dipped in ink.

Life-cycle: Unlike the Small Skipper, the eggs of this species remain unhatched through the winter until the following spring. The caterpillars feed until June, then pupate, and the adult butterflies emerge in June or July, flying until August in a single generation.

Larval Foodplants: Various coarse grasses, such as cock's foot (*Dactylis glomerata*), timothy (*Pleun pratense*), and creeping soft-grass (*Holcus mollis*).

General Remarks: Since its introduction there in about 1910, this native European species has become a pest of hayfields in some parts of the United States and Canada.

Silver-Spotted Skipper *Hesperia comma*

Family: Hesperiidae

Habitat: Dry grassy areas with fine, floriferous turf, usually on hilly limestone.

Distribution: Occurs throughout much of Europe, except for parts of the north and east, and patchily across temperate Asia. It also occurs locally in North America.

Description: A small butterfly, with a wingspan of 29–35mm ($1\frac{1}{8}$–$1\frac{1}{3}$ inches). It is generally similar in size and shape to the Small and Essex Skippers, but unusual in that both the upper and lower surfaces of the wings are boldly marked with silvery-white dots – hence its name.

Life-cycle: The eggs are relatively large for the size of butterfly, and shaped like tiny pudding basins. They remain throughout the winter until about April, when the greyish-green caterpillars hatch and begin to feed. They conceal themselves in small tents made from leaves of the foodplant and feed mainly at night. The adults appear in June or July, flying until August in one generation only.

Larval Foodplants: Fine-leaved grasses, particularly sheep's fescue (*Festuca ovina*).

General Remarks: Although still common in much of Europe, this species has dramatically declined in Britain and is now confined to just a few warm, tightly-grazed chalk downlands in the south.

Butterflies

RIODINIDAE

Duke of Burgundy Fritillery *Hamearis lucina*

Family: Riodinidae

Habitat: Open woods and sheltered flowery clearings, mainly in lowlands.

Distribution: Occurs mainly in central and southern Europe, being absent from most of Scandinavia and extending eastwards to the borders of Asia. In Britain it occurs mainly in the warmer parts of England.

Description: A small butterfly with a wingspan of 28–32mm (1–1$\frac{1}{4}$ inches), it is only the size of some of the blue butterflies (p. 38 *et seq.*), but has the markings of a fritillary; however, it is not actually related to either. The upper surfaces of the wings are dark brown with a pattern of orange dots; underneath, they are broadly similar except for the two bands of white dots.

Life-cycle: The pale dome-shaped eggs are laid in clusters of two to five under the leaves of the foodplant, hatching after about a month into hairy brown caterpillars. In northern areas there is just one brood, with adults on the wing in May and June; further south, there are usually two broods between May and September. The winter is passed in pupal form, hidden among dead leaves.

Larval Foodplants: Most frequently cowslips (*Primula veris*), less frequently primroses (*Primula vulgaris*).

General remarks: Known as the Duke of Burgundy Fritillary due to its fritillary-like appearance, it is actually the only European representative of a mainly tropical family.

Moths

SATURNIIDAE

Indian Moon-Moth *Actias selene*

Family: Saturniidae

Habitat: Most frequent in open woodland, less often around parks and gardens.

Distribution: Southern parts of Asia, especially India, Sri Lanka, southern China, Indonesia and Malaysia.

Description: Large, with a wingspan of 80–120mm (3$\frac{1}{4}$–4$\frac{3}{4}$ inches), it is often described, not unreasonably, as one of the most beautiful of all moths. When newly-emerged it is a lovely pale emerald green, with yellow lines and a bi-colored eye-spot on each wing. Perhaps the most distinctive feature is its shape, the hindwings being curved and prolonged into long narrow 'tails'. As with most moths, the antennae of the males are feathery, while those of the female are less branched.

Life-cycle: The caterpillars are spiny, red at first then becoming green, with brown heads and legs. In the warmest parts of the range the butterflies are on the wing continuously, though further north there are just two broods, in the warmest parts of the year. They are habitually nocturnal.

Larval Foodplants: In the wild, they appear to feed on a wide range of different plants, including species of *Hibiscus*, *Coriaria*, and *Salix*, though in captivity they eat many other shrubs.

General Remarks: The great beauty of fresh specimens and the fact that it is easy to maintain makes it is one of the most popular species in private collections.

Atlas Moth *Attacus atlas*

Family: Saturniidae

Habitat: Forests and lightly wooded areas.

Distribution: From Sri Lanka and India eastwards into south China, Malaysia and Indonesia.

Description: An enormous moth with a wingspan of 160–300mm (6$\frac{1}{4}$–12 inches), and even larger specimens have occasionally been recorded. Although there are a few moths with wings almost as long as this species, none have wings that are anywhere near as large, and it is usually accepted as the largest moth in the world, the female being distinctly larger than the male. The wings are richly patterned with chocolate brown, cream, white and red, edged with broad brownish bands, and with buff-coloured hook-tips to the forewings.

Life-cycle: As might be expected, the caterpillars are also impressively large, growing to 100mm (4 inches) in length, and over 20mm ($\frac{3}{4}$ inch) in diameter. They are green, dotted with brown and covered with warts. The adults are on the wing for most of the year in their warm, tropical environment, flying almost exclusively at night and remaining hidden by day.

Larval Foodplants: The caterpillars feed on a wide range of trees and shrubs.

General Remarks: This moth varies considerably in size and markings over its range, and some authorities have separated it into several species. It is protected by law in some countries.

Emperor Moth *Saturnia pavonia*

Family: Saturniidae

Habitat: Heathland, moors and open and unspoiled lightly-wooded areas, including estuarine woodland.

Distribution: Widespread throughout virtually the whole of Europe except for high mountain areas and the hottest and driest regions. It also extends eastwards across temperate Asia to Siberia.

Description: A medium to large moth, with a wingspan of 50–70mm (2–2¾ inches). The forewings are marbled with grey-brown and orange, edged with pale bands; but the most distinctive feature is a large 'peacock' eye-spot in the centre of each wing. The hindwings are brighter, with more orange colouring in the male. Males and females are similar in pattern, though they differ in colour, with females lacking the orange on the hindwings, which is replaced by grey.

Life-cycle: At first, the caterpillars are black with orange spots, but they gradually become conspicuously greener with black dots. The cocoon in which they pass the winter is an impressive structure, spun by the larvae, with an ingenious one-way trap-door that allows the emerging moth out while preventing parasites from entering. The adults are on the wing from April to June; males are day-flying and very mobile while females are more sedentary and nocturnal.

Larval Foodplants: Various shrubs, including heathers (*Erica* spp.), blackthorn (*Prunus spinosa*) and bramble (*Rubus fruticosus*).

General Remarks: The male has feathery, multi-branched antennae which allows it to detect tiny quantities of the female's scent and locate her over considerable distances, up to 2 miles (3 km) away.

Great Peacock Moth or Viennese Emperor
Saturnia pyri

Family: Saturniidae

Habitat: Lightly wooded areas, scrub, open forests, parks and larger gardens.

Distribution: Southern Europe from southern Germany and northern France southwards, extending east into western Asia.

Description: A large moth by European standards, with a wingspan of 100–150mm (4–6 inches). The colours and patterns on the wings are very similar to those of the Emperor Moth (p. 95), though the hindwings are greyer, with more distinct pale-yellowish margins. The main difference, however, is the size.

Life-cycle: The caterpillars are black at first, eventually becoming very large and greenish-yellow, with bright blue warts. They feed through to late summer, pupating for the winter in autumn in the upper branches of the foodplant trees. The adults are on the wing during May and June, in one generation only, and both sexes are nocturnal.

Larval Foodplants: Apple trees (*Malus* spp.), both wild and cultivated, are the favoured foodplant, though blackthorn (*Prunus spinosa*), elms (Ulmus spp.), and other trees and shrubs are used. Occasionally a pest of orchards, the moth has generally declined in recent years.

General Remarks: This is the largest moth or butterfly in Europe, and is immediately recognizable.

Life-cycle: In their early stages the caterpillars are covered with fine red spines, but these gradually disappear as the caterpillars grow, when they become large and green, with white stripes along their sides. They spend the winter as pupae, protected by tough brown cocoons. The adults are on the wing, in a single generation, between March and early June, the males flying by day, particularly in the mornings, and the females flying solely at night.

Larval Foodplants: Beech is the favoured foodplant, though other trees and shrubs such as oaks (*Quercus* spp.), hawthorns (*Crataegus* spp.), birches (*Betula* spp.) and apples (*Malus* spp.) may be used.

General Remarks: The males may fly considerable distances in search of the sedentary females, using their highly sensitive antennae to detect them. They are rather territorial and will fight off other males.

Tau Emperor or Nail-Mark Moth *Aglia tau*

Family: Saturniidae

Habitat: Deciduous woodlands, especially beech woods or where there is a high proportion of beech.

Distribution: Widespread through the central parts of Europe, extending southwards as far as northern Spain and north Italy, and northwards into southern Scandinavia, though absent from Britain. It also extends right across temperate Asia as far as Japan.

Description: A medium to large moth, with a wingspan of 55–90mm ($2\frac{1}{4}$–$3\frac{1}{2}$ inches). It is a beautiful moth, especially when newly-emerged, with yellowish-brown wings in the centre of which are eye-spots; these are normally blue, edged with black, and with a white mark in the centre (the 'nail-mark'), though over its whole range there is considerable variation in colour, and many subspecies have been described.

Moths

ARCTIIDAE

Scarlet Tiger *Callimorpha dominula*

Family: Arctiidae

Habitat: Most frequent in damp woods and fens, though may occasionally occur in drier sites such as roadsides and cliff-tops.

Distribution: Throughout most of Europe, including southern Britain, though absent from the extreme south and northern Scandinavia. It extends eastwards into temperate west Asia.

Description: A medium-sized moth with a wingspan of 45–55mm (1³/₄–2¹/₄ inches), the forewings are bluish-black, prominently dotted with large yellow or white spots in a variable pattern. The underwings are quite different – bright scarlet with black markings – and are often invisible when the moth is at rest. Males and females are similar in colour.

Life-cycle: The creamy-white eggs are laid in batches on the foodplant and soon hatch into grey and yellow spiny caterpillars, that often feed openly. The winter is passed in caterpillar form, with pupation taking place in spring, the adults emerging in June. There is one generation, on the wing between June and August.

Larval Foodplants: Comfrey (*Symphytum officionale*) is the favoured foodplant, though stinging nettles (*Urtica dioica*), dead nettles (*Lamium* spp.), and various other plants are used.

General Remarks: This species often flies by day, as well as at night, its bright warning colours affording it some protection from predators.

Jersey Tiger *Euplagia quadripunctaria*

Family: Arctiidae

Habitat: Occurs in a wide variety of habitats, but particularly in lightly wooded areas on limestone, especially near water. In Britain, it is a coastal species occurring mainly on cliff-tops and along seashores.

Distribution: Throughout most of Europe, except for Scandinavia, and eastwards into western Asia.

Description: A medium-sized moth, with a wingspan of 50–60mm (2–2½ inches). As with the Scarlet Tiger and most tiger moths, the forewings and hindwings are quite different. In this species the forewings are black, boldly striped with cream or yellow, while the underwings are orange-red with black dots.

Life-cycle: The yellowish eggs are laid in batches, hatching into larvae in early autumn. Winter is passed in caterpillar form and they resume feeding in spring, until May, when they pupate. The adults are on the wing, in a single generation, from June until September, and are often active during the day when they can be easily mistaken for butterflies.

Larval Foodplants: A wide range of species, including stinging nettles (*Urtica dioica*), dandelions (*Taraxacum officionale*), dead nettles (*Lamium* spp.), and many other herbs and small shrubs.

General Remarks: The species is famous for its large midsummer gatherings, when huge numbers congregate to aestivate (spend the summer in a state of torpor) in southern Europe. The most famous site is the so-called 'valley of butterflies' on the island of Rhodes in Greece.

Garden Tiger *Arctia caja* (pictured right)

Family: Arctiidae

Habitat: Occupies a wide range of habitats, including damp wooded valleys and fens, parks, gardens and open woodland.

Distribution: Widespread through Europe as far north as Lapland, and eastwards across Asia as far as Japan. It is also common in North America.

Description: A medium-sized moth, with a wingspan of 50–70mm (2–2³/₄ inches). The forewings are attractively patterned with brown, with interlocking broad white lines, while the underwings are bright orange-red with large bluish-black dots. A number of colour variations exist.

Life-cycle: The eggs are laid in large batches on the foodplants, hatching in early autumn to pass the winter as small caterpillars. They feed avidly in the following spring, developing into the familiar 'woolly bear' caterpillars, covered with long yellowish spines. The single generation of adults emerge in July, remaining on the wing until late August or early September, and flying almost entirely at night.

Larval Foodplants: The caterpillars feed on a very wide range of herbaceous plants and small shrubs, including nettles (*Urtica dioica*), dandelions (*Taraxacum officionale*), comfrey (*Symphytum officionale*) and many others.

General Remarks: The Garden Tiger is poisonous to most predators and advertises the fact with its bright warning colours and by certain displays, some of which may involve sound. Some of the toxins are passed on from poisonous foodplants, but the moth can also produce toxins of its own.

Cinnabar Moth *Tyria jacobaeae* (pictured right)

Family: Arctiidae

Habitat: Occurs in a wide range of open grassy locations with abundant flowers, including parks, gardens and waste ground, though not on very heavy soils where the larvae would find it difficult to burrow in order to pupate.

Distribution: Confined to Europe, apart from northern Scandinavia, where it is very widespread and generally prolific.

Description: A smallish moth, with a wingspan of 30–45mm (1¹/₄–1³/₄ inches). Its colour and pattern is unlike that of any other moth in its area of distribution. The forewings are greyish-black with broad red stripes along the front margins and two red spots towards each edge; the hindwings are mainly red with narrow blackish borders. Males and females are very similar.

Life-cycle: Eggs are laid in batches on the foodplant in midsummer and soon hatch into caterpillars which feed gregariously until early autumn. The older larvae are highly distinctive, being radially striped with black and yellow in a pattern which warns predators of their unpalatability, and they feed openly during the day. It is a curious fact that when they were introduced into New Zealand to control a certain weed, the local birds seemed unaware of the meaning of these warning colours and avidly consumed them with no apparent ill effect. Adults are on the wing from May until August, flying mainly at night but sometimes flying briefly during the day.

Larval Foodplants: Most commonly ragwort, groundsel and related species of *Senecio*. The caterpillars frequently strip their hosts of all their leaves.

General Remarks: A wide range of colour variations can occur, including moths that are all red.

Moths

NOTODONTIDAE

Pine Processionary Moth
Thaumetopoea pityocampa

Family: Notodontidae

Habitat: Pinewoods and other coniferous forests.

Distribution: Confined to central and southern Europe and adjacent areas of west Asia and north Africa. Within Europe, it extends northwards as far as central France.

Description: A small to medium moth, with a wingspan of 38–50mm (1½–2 inches). The adult moths are rather dull with brownish-white wings marked with greyish-brown streaks and dots. The caterpillars and larval tents are much more distinctive, however, the larvae feeding together in substantial and conspicuous silken tents hung from pine branches. The caterpillars emerge in procession, head to tail, to feed at night and when ready to pupate descend to the ground, again in a long procession (*see below*). It is at this stage that they are at their most noticeable – hence their common name.

Life-cycle: The eggs are laid in batches which overwinter, hatching into caterpillars that feed communally, as described above. The caterpillars themselves are bluish-black with long hairs. The adults are on the wing in May and June, with one generation per year, flying only by night.

Larval Foodplants: Pines and related conifers.

General Remarks: The famous French entomologist, Jean Henri Fabre (1823-1915), in experiments with the caterpillars of these types of moths, placed them on a flowerpot where they continued in a circle, one behind the other, until exhausted.

Moths

ZYGAENIDAE

Six-Spot Burnet *Zygaena filipendulae*

Family: Zygaenidae

Habitat: All kinds of rough grassy areas with flowers.

Distribution: Throughout most of Europe, except for the far north and the extreme south-west. It also extends eastwards into western Asia.

Description: A smallish moth, with a wingspan of 25–40mm (1–1$\frac{1}{2}$ inches). The forewings are a dark charcoal grey with six symmetrically-placed red spots on each wing. The hindwings are plain red, edged with blackish-grey and the antennae are long, broadening out towards the tips.

Life-cycle: The eggs are laid in late summer and soon hatch into caterpillars which overwinter and recommence feeding in spring. When mature, they are yellowish-green dotted with black in lines. They pupate in early summer, and the adults emerge in June, flying until August, in one brood. They fly mainly by day, in a weak fluttery manner, and may be confused with butterflies. The papery cocoons from which the moths emerge remain conspicuously attached to grass stems long after they are empty.

Larval Foodplants: Various low-growing leguminous plants such as bird's foot trefoil (*Lotus corniculatus*).

General Remarks: There are many similar species with various numbers of spots or arrangements of red on their forewings.

Moths

SPHINGIDAE

Broad-Bordered Bee Hawkmoth
Hemaris fuciformis

Family: Sphingidae

Habitat: Most frequent in woodland clearings, rides and margins, though also occurring in more open flowery locations such as alpine meadows.

Distribution: Throughout most of Europe (except for northern Scandinavia and most of Spain), into north Africa and eastwards into west Asia.

Description: A smallish moth, with a wingspan of 38–43mm ($1^{1}/_{2}$–$1^{3}/_{4}$ inches). The wings are clear, edged with brownish-red and veined with black. The body is large in relation to the wings, covered with brownish hairs except for a reddish band around the 'waist' and two black spots near the tip. It does

resemble a bumble-bee to some extent, reinforced by the fact that it is mainly abroad by day.

Life-cycle: The eggs are singly laid on the undersides of leaves. They hatch in midsummer, and the caterpillars feed through until August, becoming large and green, dotted with red, and with short horns at one end. They pass the winter as pupae and the adults emerge in April or May. In the south, there may be a smaller second generation later in the summer.

Larval Foodplants: Honeysuckle (*Lonicera periclymenum*), various bedstraws (*Galium* spp.), and sometimes the introduced snowberries (*Symphoricarpos* spp.).

General Remarks: This attractive little moth flies by day, particularly in the mornings, regularly visiting flowers such as bugle (*Ajuga reptans*) and rhododendrons. It has a faster, more darting flight than than that of a bumble-bee.

Death's Head Hawkmoth *Acherontia atropos*

Family: Sphingidae

Habitat: A mobile and strongly migratory species that can occur almost anywhere. Because the eggs are laid on potatoes and members of the nightshade family, the females are more than likely to be seen where these plants are present.

Distribution: Southern Europe and northern Africa, but migration occurs outwards from this area each summer, extending well into northern Europe and western Asia.

Description: A large moth, with a wingspan of 100–140mm (4–5$\frac{1}{2}$ inches), it is a most distinctive species, not only because of its size but also because of its markings. The forewings are a deep blue-black, marbled with paler colours, while the hindwings are yellowish, striped with black. The body is very broad, similar in colour to the hindwings, except for the skull-like markings (the death's head) just behind the head.

Life-cycle: Eggs are laid in batches on the foodplants, hatching into caterpillars that may eventually reach some 120mm (4$\frac{3}{4}$ inches) in length. They are green or brown, and feed only at night. Adults move northwards in early summer, flying only at night, and may produce one, or even two generations in more northerly parts of the range, but will inevitably fail to survive the winter. Pupation takes place in an earthen cocoon, deep in the soil.

Larval Foodplants: Potatoes, woody and deadly nightshades and other members of the species *Solanum*.

General Remarks: These enormous moths regularly visit beehives to take honey when they make curious squeaking sounds which are thought to quieten the bees and prevent them from attacking. Not surprisingly, many superstitions are associated with such an unusual insect.

Eyed Hawkmoth *Smerinthus ocellata*

Family: Sphingidae

Habitat: Lightly wooded areas, river valleys, parks, gardens and orchards.

Distribution: Throughout central and northern Europe and eastwards across much of temperate Asia, excluding Japan.

Description: A large moth, with a wingspan of 70–85mm ($2^3/_4$–$3^1/_3$ inches). The forewings are brown, marbled with lighter shades and resemble dead leaves. The hindwings, which are usually concealed, are reddish, with enormous black-ringed eye-spots. When disturbed, the moth will give a quick flash of its underwings, then quickly return them to the camouflaged closed-wing position; this causes potential predators to back off before losing sight of the moth altogether.

Life-cycle: The eggs are laid in early summer, soon hatching into caterpillars which feeds voraciously throughout the summer. When fully grown, they are large and pale green, with bluish horns at one end. They pass the winter in the soil as pupae, and the adult moths emerge in May, flying until July. From year to year, and in some areas, there may be a second generation later in the summer. Unless disturbed, the adults fly only at night.

Larval Foodplants: A variety of shrubs and trees, including apples (*Malus* spp.), willows (*Salix* spp.), poplars (*Populus* spp.), aspen (*P. tremula*) and plums (*Prunus* spp.).

General Remarks: The caterpillars, though so striking when seen out of context, are a fine example of camouflage thanks to the subtle countershading, with the upper surface darker than the lower, balanced out when the direction of the light is from above. Upside-down, they are far more noticeable.

Spurge Hawkmoth *Hyles euphorbiae*

Family: Sphingidae

Habitat: Sand-dunes, dry hillsides, scrub and light woodland or woodland margins.

Distribution: Southern Europe, from where it migrates annually into the less favourable climates of central and northern Europe or adjacent parts of west Asia. Introduced into Canada to help control weedy spurges, it is now well established there.

Description: With a span of 80–90mm ($3\frac{1}{8}$–$3\frac{1}{2}$ inches), the forewings are attractively marbled with olive-green, grey and lighter shades, while the hindwings are broadly striped with red, black and white. As with most hawkmoths, the bodies are broad, and striped with black, white and brown.

Life-cycle: The caterpillars are most flamboyant in varying patterns of green, red, black and white, with single black-tipped red horns. They feed openly on their foodplants, protected by their warning colours which are reinforced by the presence of toxins stored in their bodies, transferred to them from the foodplant. The first generation of adults is on the wing in early summer, and in southern areas there is a second brood later on. They migrate northwards each year, flying at night, but fail to survive winter.

Larval Foodplants: Various species of spurge (*Euphorbia*), especially sea-spurge and cypress spurge.

General Remarks: This is possibly the most common hawkmoth in southern Europe.

Striped Hawkmoth *Hyles lineata*

Family: Sphingidae

Habitat: A strong-flying moth that migrates widely, it can therefore occur in almost any habitat, particularly where there are open, flowery spaces.

Distribution: The most widespread of any species of hawkmoth, it can be regularly seen throughout the United States and Canada, in Central America, across much of Africa, most of Europe, and the temperate parts of Asia. It also occurs in Australia. It migrates outwards from its strongholds in the warmer temperate regions.

Description: A moderate to large moth, with a wingspan of 70–80mm ($2\frac{3}{4}$–$3\frac{1}{8}$ inches). 'Striped' is a good description of this insect, as that is the overriding impression it conveys: the forewings are brownish, striped with paler colours, and there are two clear whitish stripes on the body behind the head. The underwings are pink, edged with brown and white.

Life-cycle: The large, brightly-coloured caterpillars grow rapidly and at least two generations of moths are produced in most parts of the range, more if conditions permit. The moths migrate outwards from their favoured breeding areas when numbers begin to rise, flying by night and day, often in huge groups. They fail to survive the winters in these peripheral regions, but the process is nonetheless repeated again the following year.

Larval Foodplants: A wide range of plants may be used, including willow-herbs (*Epilobium* spp.), bedstraws (*Galium* spp.), fuchsias, docks (*Rumex* spp.), and vines (*Vitis vinifera*).

General Remarks: At dusk and throughout the night, the adults visit various flowers such as tobacco plants (*Nicotiana* spp.) and honeysuckles (*Lonicera* spp.), gathering nectar.

Oleander Hawkmoth *Daphnis nerii*

Family: Sphingidae

Habitat: Normally in river valleys and any place where oleanders grow, but it is a highly mobile species that can occur almost anywhere.

Distribution: Its main breeding areas are the extreme south of Europe, southern temperate Asia eastwards into India, and northern Africa; but it migrates northwards from these areas every year, failing to survive the winters.

Description: A large moth, with a wingspan of 80–120mm ($3^1/_8$–$4^3/_4$ inches). The forewings have a beautiful marbled pattern of pink, greenish-brown and cream, with two small eye-spots close to the body. The hindwings are smaller and less highly-coloured.

Life-cycle: The caterpillars feed in loose groups, eventually attaining a length of 150mm (6 inches). They are impressive creatures, olive-green in colour with blue eye-spots and black-tipped yellow horns. In the warmer parts of the range there are several broods throughout the summer, and in most years migrations take place from May onwards to northern parts of Europe, including Britain, though this is a rare occurrence. If suitable foodplants are available the moths may breed in these northern areas, but inevitably fail to survive for very long.

Larval Foodplants: Most frequently oleanders, but also species of periwinkle (*Vinca*), and occasionally vines.

General Remarks: Although it feeds mainly on poisonous plants, the toxins are not transferred to the caterpillar or adult. Its appearance is more for camouflage than warning.

Elephant Hawkmoth *Deilephila elpenor*

Family: Sphingidae

Habitat: Occurs in a variety of habitats, including waste land, parks, gardens, woodland clearings and alpine pastures.

Distribution: Widespread throughout virtually the whole of Europe, and eastwards across temperate Asia as far as Japan.

Description: Of medium size, with a wingspan of 58–65mm ($2\frac{1}{4}$–$2\frac{1}{2}$ inches), it is a strikingly beautiful insect; the wings are broadly striped with pinkish-grey and golden-brown, and the broad furry body is golden brown with longitudinal pink stripes. The antennae are large and white. The Small Elephant Hawkmoth (*D. porcellus*) is similar though smaller, the wing-striping being less defined.

Life-cycle: The caterpillars are impressive when fully grown, greenish or brownish, with two sets of eye-spots behind the head; when threatened they are able to withdraw their heads and enlarge the eye-spots to produce dramatic, threatening displays. The caterpillars feed through the late summer and overwinter as pupae. The adults are on the wing between May and July in one generation, abroad almost entirely at night.

Larval Foodplants: Willowherbs (*Epilobium* spp.), especially rose-bay willowherb, are the commonest foodplants, though fuchsias, bedstraws (*Galium* spp.) and other plants are used.

General Remarks: One of the most common and most frequently encountered hawkmoths of Britain and northern Europe.